63615

Checked 13/03/11 JH

£12·50

93

994

00

1·677

The Year 'Round

The Year 'Round

Guy Wheeler

ILLUSTRATIONS BY PETER BIEGEL

Gentry Books: London

Published by Gentry Books Limited,
55-61, Moorgate, London, EC2R 6BR

Printed photolitho in Great Britain by
Ebenezer Baylis and Son Limited,
The Trinity Press,
Worcester, and London

For Stephanie

Foreword

I t w a s a good many years ago that I first met Guy Wheeler when, as a young cavalry officer, he came to hunt with my hounds in the Portman country. It soon became evident to me that, unlike the general run of young soldiers whose main object— quite understandably—is to jump fences, Guy was intensely interested in venery and the science of Foxhunting. He wanted to know the whys and wherefores of what was going on, and being of an observant and determined nature, he made it his business to find out.

A year or two later he went still higher in my estimation when he had the good sense to marry a charming girl who was a member of one of our keenest foxhunting families.

It therefore came as no great surprise to me to learn that he had written a book about his experiences as a foxhunter, both in England and America, although I must confess that I did not anticipate that he would prove to be quite such a gifted writer! I have enjoyed reading his book immensely, even more especially since it is so beautifully illustrated by an old friend, Peter Biegel, who also hunted with me and whose fame as a sporting artist is world-wide.

I would like particularly to commend the title of his first chapter "Time Spent in Reconnaissance is Seldom Wasted". So far as Foxhunting is concerned no Master of Hounds, or Huntsman, will ever be successful if he ignores this famous military dictum. And those who ride to hounds will find, as Brigadier Wheeler has found, that by following this excellent advice they will obtain the maximum amount of enjoyment from the greatest of all sports.

Peter Farquhar

For'rard On

"FOX-'UNTERS ARE FAMOUS FELLOWS" according to Mr.
Jorrocks and none more famed than Colonel Sir Peter Farquhar,
Bt. His Masterships of the Tedworth, the Meynell, the
Whaddon Chase and the Portman are part of fox-hunting
history and legend. My gratitude now for the generosity of
his Foreword is matched only by my enjoyment when—on
horse or on foot—I have watched him hunt his hounds, or
listened to him speak of them.

Many years ago I suggested to my distinguished friend,
Peter Biegel, that if ever I should produce a book of this sort
I should ask him to illustrate it. I recall that, understandably,
he was a little diffident at the time. But when, to the surprise of
both of us, the idea became fact, he responded as one would
expect of him; immediately, wholeheartedly and generously.

I record here my gratitude for his collaboration and my admiration for his artistry.

In writing the last section of the final chapter and entitling it "Try Back" I had two motives.

Firstly, I intended it as my grateful compliment to fox-hunting in America, and to those American foxhunters through whose phenomenal generosity I enjoyed three seasons of hunting in an amazing variety of temperatures, weathers, going and circumstances never to be experienced in this country. It was these friends who introduced me to hunting terms which at first seemed foreign until I realised that they were the older English usages now grown out of favour on this side of the Atlantic. And introduced me too—in some of their backwoods country—to forms of hunting gloriously reminiscent of the remarkable chase described by Surtees in the first chapter in "Handley Cross", entitled "The Olden Times", where the appearance and jealous individualism of the nondescript rabble of trencher-fed hounds tallies with the enthusiastic eccentricities of their owners. The piece is not uncritical of American fox-hunting. But acquaintance with Americans has taught me that they look for constructive criticism from their friends—sometimes even a little too earnestly.

Secondly, I intended the title as an exhortation to some of the English hunting community—only some; the message supporting the exhortation being contained in the closing two paragraphs.

Before I am hotly criticised on both sides of the Atlantic for my criticism of both sides, on the grounds that I have based it on my own limited experience and personal prejudices, may I say that no fewer than three highly respected Masters of Foxhounds—Mr. William W. Brainard, Jr., Master of the Old Dominion of Hounds of Virginia, Major Charles Kindersley, Master of the Eglinton Hounds of Ontario and Major Robert Hoare, then Master of the Cottesmore Hounds of

Rutland, were all kind enough to advise me in the writing of it and to comment on the final draft. I am grateful to all three for the authority their advice has conferred upon its conclusions. But the conclusions are my own.

You will observe, that in arranging the order of the first twelve chapters I have departed from the conventional progression of the Gregorian calendar and begun with the month of September. Most English packs begin cub-hunting in August, but in America very few make a start before October. So, I compromised by taking September as representing the opening month of the season.

But whatever the date, I believe for everyone the hunting season begins when, with a perfunctory tap at the barometer, one says—

"They're meeting at six-thirty tomorrow at the bottom of the hill. I think I'll take the mare. She could do with a bit more work now. We'd better keep her in to-night. . . ."

The following sketches in this book were originally published in the journals shown below. "Conflict of Loyalties," *The Times* and *The Maryland Horse*; "Early One Morning" and "To Close the Season," *The Field* and *The Maryland Horse*; "Not Saint Andrew's Day," *Riding* and *The Maryland Horse*; "The Opening Meet," "One Christmas Eve," and "See Amid the Winter Snow," *The Maryland Horse*, "Try Back," *The Field* and *The Chronicle of the Horse*.

CONTENTS

xiii

The Year 'Round

Time Spent in Reconnaissance
is Seldom Wasted

I CANNOT SAY for certain who was originally responsible for this military maxim. I shouldn't think it was Alexander the Great; he was always one for pressing on regardless. I suspect it might have been Julius Caesar whose orthodox and deliberate tactics and insistence on a sound logistical backing for any campaign make him a much more likely character. Alexander might have made an excellent Master of Fox Hounds in the English 'Shires, so long as he had a good huntsman to get him out of the occasional mess. Caesar, I expect would have been a good Master anywhere though possibly a shade too circumspect for the thrusters; but he could certainly have dealt effectively with the over-eager.

However, my point is that whoever claims to have originated the epigram could have equally intended it as an instruction for

B

3

Masters of Hounds, especially those intending to hunt hounds themselves.

To quote Sir Charles Frederick, Bt., once Master of the Pytchley,

"The days are past, if indeed they ever existed, when a Master of Hounds could turn his back on the country of his adoption during the summer months. This surely is the time when the foundations of his future sport are laid, and if they be not well and truly laid, no eleventh hour efforts are likely to avail when the first of November is in sight. Till the country is learnt by heart and a pretty comprehensive knowledge gained of the dwellers therein, a Master of Hounds is in no condition to take the field, and it is plain knowledge enough that his task is mastered only at the cost of hard work."

This will be a novel concept to many who have laboured under the delusion that the responsibilities of a Master were confined primarily to dancing at the Hunt Ball with the wives of all the more difficult landowners in his country, admittedly, no lightly discharged responsibility in itself; and secondly, damning the eyes of anyone who pressed hounds too hard, being ever ready to crush the thruster's complaint of —

"I didn't come out here to be damned, sir!" with the coup de grace—

"Then go home and be damned, sir!"

A Master has certain other obligations which demand his closest attention and not least of these is the need to comply with Sir Charles Frederick's injunctions to learn his country and, at the same time, gain "a pretty comprehensive knowledge of the dwellers therein."

However, it was never my intention to instruct my Masters. But merely to point out that a Master's duty can well be a Hunt Member's delight. For a keen fox-hunter with time to spare in the summer there can be few more enjoyable—or more eventually profitable—occupations than to conduct a number of recon-

Badger Setts

naissances at leisure, on foot, on horse and by car, through the country where in the coming winter he will hunt.

By car he can find the best ways to the meets and the most convenient places to park and unload his horsebox; invaluable knowledge when time is short—and I've never known it otherwise on a hunting day.

On horseback he can learn the run of the rides through the woods through which hounds will draw; he can memorise the short cuts to avoid the more time-consuming defiles—and the more disconcerting obstacles—and to get to the hounds quickly when he is left on the one side of the covert with the pack smartly away on the other on the line of a fast travelling fox. He can note where the new growth in a hedge has plaited the old rusted, stop-gap wire into a treacherous, hidden snare for any idle jumper given to taking his chances through the tops of his fences. He can mark where the jagged teeth and links of an ancient broken chain harrow, long discarded and forgotten under the lea of a hedgerow, awaits the unwary. No farmer will ever object to being advised of these hazards; especially if the adviser offers at the same time to arrange for their removal.

On foot, he can establish the best vantage points from which to view a cover; the easiest way through, or round, a perennial thorn bullfinch; the surest footing along the banks of a stream and the best places to jump it, and—always useful to know—the probable depth if he lands in the middle, with or without his horse.

These and many other such items worth remembering, he can with advantage learn in anticipation of the perils and contingencies attendant upon the fox-hunter in the field. At the same time, and indeed, all the time, he can learn the lie, the habits and the runs of the animals, and in particular of the foxes. The location of open rabbit burrows, badger setts, drains, hollow trees, disused and overgrown quarries and old deserted huts and houses—all these can serve as earths and refuges for a hunted fox, and if known or remarked to be regularly used are worth a mental note. Foxes, like any other animals, including man, are creatures of habit. Their movements are primarily dictated by their need to eat and to mate. To achieve these aims they prefer, being no less idle than their human counterparts, to use the variety of well defined paths travelled regularly by all the other animals of the countryside; appreciating that no useful purpose is achieved by ploughing solitarily through the bottom of the one part of a thick thorn hedge if, ten yards along, the rabbits have worn a neat hole in it during their travels to the clover field. Hunting or hunted, the fox will use the rabbits' gap and similar convenient ways known to him and all the other animals of the area. With the summer-gained knowledge of the "fauna freeways"—though the winter movement of animals does not always exactly coincide with their movement by summer—and the memory of how the fox ran the last time a particular covert was drawn, together with a note of the direction of the wind and an acquaintance with the adjacent countryside, the Hunt Member is well capable of ensuring not only that he gets to hounds himself, but even may assist the Field Master in getting there as well.

In many hunting households it is a regular practice to record on one of those excellent hunting maps, the date, time and route of every notable hunt. These are always of interest and of considerable assistance to a better knowledge of a country, though their detail and the hunting information they give should be checked against the existing situation. New roads, new building, deforestation and the like alterations to the face of the land will probably deter a fox from taking what appears from former recorded occasions to be the habitual vulpine escape route out of a particular area. A lot of amusement may be had on a winter's evening, after a day on which hounds have scored some memorable run, comparing the day's performance with records of earlier runs from the same covert.

Beside all this, whilst quietly and unobtrusively learning the country, our Hunt Member can meet the people who live in it. He can meet the farmers over whose land he will ride. He will meet the tractor driver, the shepherd, the cowman, the roadman, the gamekeeper and the policeman and a host of others. They will be able to tell him where a vixen lies with her cubs, and whether that old dog fox they lost last year down by the river is still living in the hollow tree below the bridge. They will be the ones who during the season will help him to find hounds, will advise him on the line of the hunted fox. They will open and close the gates for him. They will hold his horse whilst he dismounts to examine a cut or a strain; or his head whilst, after some crucifying jerk, he lies prostrate wondering whether it is still attached to his body. They will ever be ready to greet him and pass the time of day when a chance meeting and time allows. For these are the true countryfolk, part of the countryside, for whom the hunting of the fox is an essential feature in their own personal sporting calendar.

From these men he will discover which fields will be under seed and which lie fallow in the coming season; which pastures will be ploughed and which hedges trimmed down or taken out altogether; which rides will be cleared in the woods and what timber will be cut or what areas will be planted out, altering the extent and character of a covert. All these points are useful guides to anyone wishing to stay with hounds and watch them work to best advantage; and, with this knowledge, he will be the more able to offer effective help to the hunt staff should the need arise.

And all the time and on every 'reconnaissance' he will need to remember that the countryside as he sees it in summer and early autumn will be strangely transformed by November, after the first frosts have shrivelled the tall weeds and stripped the leaves off bush and tree, baring the secret labyrinths of the thorn thickets. The hedges stand starker, the rides lie broader, the ditches deeper, wider and blacker. The countryside will seem raw-boned, more open, sparer. And the darkness of the turned soil, the dulled shading of fern and briar drained of the clarity of their summer colouring, will blur in confused contrast the uncertain line where ditch and hedgerow meet.

He will need to remember that the fitful warmth of the winter sun will early shroud the hillsides and vales in mist, distorting his view and deadening the cry of hounds in the still air.

All this he will need to picture to himself as he stands in the full sun on the hill, while all the lushness of the vale spreads before him, and the soft sounds and scents of summer surround him.

OCTOBER

Early One Morning

THE MASTER SAID, "Six-thirty tomorrow morning at Ashmore cross-roads, and I'm not waiting for anyone. The weather people say it's going to be hot tomorrow."

"Starting a bit earlier this year?"

"Well, can't ever start too early, especially with a big new entry. Can't do any damage round Ashmore so long as we stick to the Copse and the Sixpenny Hangings. Do we see you then?"

"I'll be there," I said.

It was one of those stuffy, airless mornings with the sun an ugly orange through the haze. No wind and nothing moved. Not a bird spoke, save a pigeon in the beeches commenting on the dawn with a hoarse, burbling coo as he turned over and put his head back under the blankets.

A quick cup of coffee, biscuits crammed in the pocket and a moment's agony as the mare, overfresh from her summering, tramples my foot as I adjust her throat-lash. Up, wondering how many bones are broken in my numbed foot, and away on the four-mile hack to the cross-roads.

The mare plunges and jogs and spooks and snorts, still soft and awkward from being long unridden. The sweat dribbles from my browband into my eyes and down my cheek; my stock clings stickily round my throat. But as we descend the hill the valley mist suddenly strikes chill, the dew hangs a silver edging on the leaves and the vapour coils in the branches.

Hounds have just arrived when I reach the cross-roads and, true to his word, the Master moves off at once.

Ashmore Copse is a long finger of wood, crooked inside the curve of Sixpenny Hill, the ridge of down which shields Ashmore village from the north-east winds.

The Master makes his dispositions. To me—

"Get along to the bottom end, Guy, down by the holly trees on the old coach road there. There's some gaps in the hedge they can get through over the road and down to the withy beds. You won't be able to watch them all—I'll send someone along to help you as soon as I've got anyone."

I swing open the roadside gate and trot soundlessly along the grass track beside the wood. The close turf covers the river road along which the coaches rolled to Shaston in the old days. Of the holly trees, customarily planted along the verges to show by their dense blackness the width of the road at night, only a few at the far end of the copse remain. These hang over the track from a briar-crowned bank and in the thorns are half-a-dozen gaps.

I examine the gaps carefully and decide to wait opposite the middle one—the largest and, judging from its wear, the most used by the copse's inhabitants.

Now from the far end of the wood comes faintly yet that

sound—lovely and thrilling at any time, but loveliest when heard again for the first time in the season—the short, twanging note of the horn as hounds are put in and the high, clear call of the huntsman to his hounds, echoing through the wreathing mist and the still trees.

The sun, peering over the shoulder of the down, turns the grey mantle on the trees to golden rose. Circling high above, against a pale blue sky, the rooks swing in slow circles, their cries seeming sleepily hushed at this early hour. A mistle thrush comes bouncing along the coach road looking for its breakfast, and stops short on seeing me. It cocks its head on one side and looks hopeful. I throw it some biscuit crumbs. Startled by the fling of my arm, it flutters up and back a few paces in a flurry of wings, but comes quickly in again to take the crumbs, and is at once joined by a hen blackbird and some hedge-sparrows. I begin to think that this is one of the nicest mornings I can remember.

At this point I am joined, in a shambling run, by a fat, shaggy, disconsolate pony topped by a small boy in an old, grey hunt cap enveloping most of his head. Peering up at me under his peak, like any guardsman, he tells me, all in one breath—

"Please, sir, the Master has sent me to help you but I can't stay out for long because Mummy said that I have to be back for breakfast at half-past eight at the latest and it takes nearly three-quarters of an hour to get home and please can you tell me the right time?"

I tell him he has nearly an hour in hand, at which his pony, obviously wanting its breakfast, looks even more disconsolate, and post him opposite the far end gap.

Now the hounds speak clear in the woods. They swing from side to side of the copse, up and down and through and round. The rustle and crash as they plough through the undergrowth in

A tremendous yell from the boy

full cry sets the heart pounding. They round towards us, nearer and nearer. I try to watch all six gaps at once and both of us keep up a steady tattoo with our whips on our boots and are loud in our injunctions to any possible fox to—

"Aaarrh, ge' back in then—" only, my small companion, labouring with a man-sized whip, hits his pony more often than his leg, which does not improve its temper. It snorts and humps and props and I fear that he will inevitably disappear backwards over the road edge into the reed-bed, and hastily try to recall what it said on television about artificial respiration.

But the racket we raise seems effective. Not a hard-pressed cub essays the gaps, and, the din fading to the far end of the covert, we sit back satisfied with the results of our vigilance. I ride down to the boy to congratulate him. He thanks me politely and asks me the right time again.

"Because, Mummy told me to keep asking the right time and then I won't be late for breakfast."

I put his mind at rest and he beams happily under his frayed peak. The pony's expression remains set at stormy.

I turn to ride the fifty yards back to my chosen station and am just there when, into the thorn frame of a further gap there trots, quietly and deliberately, a fox. Seeing me it stops dead, poised on the crest of the bank. I ram the mare into a canter and roar like a bull but the fox stands its ground, slightly crouched as if about to leap down into the roadway. As I thunder up to it a tremendous yell from the boy turns me in the saddle to see two cubs, brushes a-fly, whip out of the middle gap, across the road and into the withies in a sandy streak.

Cursing, I canter on up to the fox in the gap. A full-grown vixen, she stands quite fearlessly there until I am almost up to her, elegantly evil, sleek and well groomed. The expression on her sharp little mask is one I have seen before on the face of a woman when she has got a man exactly where she wants him. It says clearly.

"Mug."

She lifts one corner of her lip, more in a smirk than a snarl, and, with an effortless, feminine grace, wheels and slides silently back into the undergrowth, to rescue the rest of her litter from the hounds.

My young aide, after his tenth enquiry as to the time, decides to disappear in the direction of his breakfast. Removing his cap in farewell he says solemnly.

"I'm very sorry, sir, I let those two get past."

"My fault entirely," I answer, "they had us both fooled. Those cubs have got a mother like yours. She knows how to look after her young."

The Opening Meet

I NEVER UNDERSTAND why it should be so, but in my household hunting mornings are always a hectic rush despite all the preparations I make the day before. This is a constant source of exasperation to my wife and amusement to my friends who, without exception, claim that their hunting mornings are tranquil pools of unruffled calm. The most chaotic morning of the season is the one of the opening meet. With horses, tack, boots, spurs and whip all gleaming; coat, breeches, gloves and hat all glossy clean the day before and every possible preparation made, still invariably and inevitably on that morning an infinite variety of mischance makes chaos come again. My alarm fails, my razor burns out, the trailer develops a flat tyre overnight. And when, finally, all obstacles overcome, I pick up my hat, gloves and whip and head for the door with twenty minutes in hand for a

half-hour's drive, one of my efficient friends calls from his tranquil pool of unruffled calm asking agitatedly if I have a spare
spur strap or martingale.

Having accomplished the half-hour's drive in fifteen frenzied
minutes, I rattle the mare out of the trailer, whip off her rug,
pull up her girth and, perspiring freely, bump down the road to
join the throng round the cross-roads where we traditionally
meet.

The clamour of tongues attains the volume of a cocktail party
as I approach and the tenour of the conversation is not dissimi-
lar. I've often wondered if the horses are saying the same sort of
things to each other. There is much greeting of acquaintances
not seen since last season, and some comment, sotto voce, on the
deterioration in their appearance; favourable comment being
made at full volume. The same jokes are made on the same
subjects. The same legs are pulled as are always extended for
the operation. Riders and foot followers mill and shift and clutter the cross-roads. The cars of the hunt supporters' club effectively block all four roads for a mile around. No one cares, least
of all the local tradesmen's van drivers, who lean out of their
cabs gossiping with anyone within earshot. The law, embodied
in the local constable on his bicycle, has been here since before
the meet, too preoccupied to tend to such mundane details as the
regulation of traffic. This is the country, and the country is
gathered at its prime annual festival—the opening meet. The
rest of the world can go hang the while; at any rate it can ruddy
well wait.

"Hounds, gentlemen, please." The words bring order to the
immobile chaos. The hitherto impenetrable mass yields like
magic, and through the narrow path, led by the first whip, his
lash hanging swaying before their eager noses, bustle the
hounds, their heads and sterns high, bright-eyed, their excitement and enthusiasm infectious. They are followed by the Master, hunting the bitch pack today, and the second whip.

❧

At a decent distance, behind the Field Master, the field range themselves into some semblance of order, to be inexorably amended by the first real obstacle into the divisions of those who go and those who don't. In the rear of the scrimmage anxious parents on steady old reliables attempt to rally their over-enthusiastic young bouncing about on their over-eager ponies. At the far back the qualifiers teeter and sidle, their riders—and probable eventual jockeys—with their knees under their chins; the horses all eyes, froth, bandages and rubber reins.

The first whip turns off the road into a field of standing kale through a gate held open by the local council roadman. The hounds follow close.

"See'd a brace in there meself this mornin', sir," the roadman calls.

"Thank you, Bert," says the Master. "Hold up, my girls, hold up then." He halts and the bitch pack crowd round his horse, wriggling, quivering and grinning. "Tom, get on up to the top end, will you."

The first whip canters on alongside the kale to the far hedge and stands so that he can watch two sides of the field. The Master turns to the Field Master.

"I don't want him over the road into the wood, George. Line it will you—and no gaps. And send someone to watch the far side."

The Field Master nods at me and I trot down the road to where a track leads off beside the kale field. If the fox breaks on my side he must cross the open track, which has deep black ditches on either side. I note that the hedge beside the kale is thickly grown to its foot with few small gaps, none of which look worn. I doubt he will come this way and look for my quickest way to hounds if he breaks on the first whip's side.

The field shuffles and shambles into a ragged series of clumps along the road. The qualifiers passage and piaffe down to the end of my track and halt there in a thin cloud of steam. I'm

I ram my hat down firmly on my head

delighted to see them there as they will effectively block the charge of the field behind me down the track if the fox breaks at the top end. Though I hate to think of the language, if this does happen.

The Master, satisfied with his dispositions, puts hounds in with a lift of his hand and a quiet "Eleu in then." They need no more encouragement. They hurl themselves into the kale and disappear like a parti-coloured wave disintegrating on a rock. The kale standing high as a man's waist, shakes and heaves above them as they plunge through. Now and again a single hound leaps high over the tops of some thicker patch dropping back through the broad leaves like a dolphin diving. Another rears on her hind legs and stands, tongue hanging, head turning, looking for the tip of some waving stern to guide her to where the action is.

A red-brown shape slips from the edge of the kale, under the roadside hedge, swerves across the road through a gap in the startled field and is up the bank and into the wood. Too late shouts echo and horses wheel and plunge. The Master turns and glares from the middle of the kale. The Field Master moves quickly to the spot. His voice has the quality of an ice saw.

"Quiet." A chilly hush. Then, "If you'd kindly stop coffee-housing and pay a little more attention to what you are asked to do we might just conceivably get a hunt." The hush gets chillier.

Just at this moment the first whip stands up in his stirrups, his gaze following the line of the hedge running away from the far side of the kale field, his hat at arms length above his head.

The Master pulls his horn from between his top buttons and begins to trot through the kale towards the far fence. In the top corner a hound speaks, distinctively high and short.

The Master lets drive.

"Yooi Ladybird. Hark to Ladybird. Hark to Ladybird all of yer. Yooi Ladybird." And his horn twangs encouragement.

Now the kale comes really alive as hounds drive through it converging on Ladybird's corner. One after another they own her line. The green crop between the corner and the gap in the hedge through which the fox had slipped disappears, flattened under their surging rush. The hedge staggers and heaves as they plunge through it or over it, and on they storm with the sound of a thousand bells, the Master's horn screaming the 'gone away' behind them.

I ram my hat down firmly on my head and push the mare into a canter along the track. A couple of hundred yards on, close under the hedge, the local gamekeeper and the tractor driver of the farm stand by a gate into a meadow. They swing it open as I come up and the gamekeeper says—

"Come through here, Colonel, and you got that hedge there. They're swinging left handed away from you."

"Thank you. Better leave the gate open, there'll be some more coming."

"You'm best watch thic big ole ditch t'other side of 'edge, Colonel," calls the tractor man, "Oi been a-clearin' 'er out and oi 'ant made 'er no smaller."

"You can pull me out with your tractor."

I gallop on across the meadow, standing up to ease the mare and sitting down again, cursing as I realise that one of my nice new stirrup leathers is stretching more than the other and unbalancing me. The mare snatches at her bit and strides on at the hedge. She sweeps cleanly over it and the great grave of a ditch with its black and stinking ridge of cleared rubbish flashes below me.

Over to my left I can see that the field have split. Some are following my line, others have gone into the kale field from the road, and, cantering in single file down the edge of the kale, are now crashing over or through the double where the Master and Tom had jumped it. A double consists of two parallel stout thorn hedges set on top of a high bank with a ditch either side. To take

it safely a horse must jump fairly slowly up over the first ditch
and hedge on to the bank, and then straight off with no change
of stride out over the far hedge and ditch. It takes a clever horse
and a confident rider to do the thing properly; a happy combination uncommon in any hunting field.

Some doubles are small enough to fly all in one. This is not
such a double. A large lady approaches it in remote control of a
large horse which is navigating its headlong course by study of
the stars. Too late the animal observes the fence though the lady
has been warning it at the top of her voice for the last fifty yards.
It heaves into the air with a hideous ungainliness, catches its
fore feet in the hedge roots and nosedives into the far ditch.
With the squeal of a failing factory hooter the large lady accom-
panies it.

"By God, she's quenched!" A voice rings out behind me.
"Poor old bag. Good job her old man's a doctor."

"Where is he? D'you think she's all right?" I take a pull at
the mare. My conscience is telling me to help, but if we stop to
pull her out of the ditch we will never see hounds again, the way
they are running.

"He's just behind her, and the way he usually goes he'll be
landing on top of her any second. No need to stop, Guy. There's
plenty of people there to help."

Hounds are rounding the corner of a small wood ahead of us.
Ben, the second whip, bringing on the tail hounds out of covert, has got left behind a little. He turns from the line the hounds
are taking and disappears over a rail into a ride through the
wood. This must be the shorter way to hounds and I decide to
follow. The mare skids on the muddy take off, rattles the rail
and pecks on landing. I sit back and let her have all the rein as
she recovers. My companion, following too close behind, checks
his horse sharply as he lands.

"Stap me! I thought my old devil was going to mount your
mare!"

We canter on down the ride and out of the wood over a bigger and blacker rail. The mare picks her feet well up this time. Behind me there is a splintering of timber, a loud oath and a louder thud. The loose horse, reins swinging against its forelegs, comes up alongside me. I catch it and trot back with it to the disconsolate pedestrian running towards me.

"Thank you," he puffs, "Very kind. Bloody fool never took off at all. Hope we haven't lost hounds."

He remounts and we gallop on. The tracks are easy to follow. Through a gap in the hedge, on to the road, along the roadside, and through a farmyard, struggling with the gates while the horses stamp and sidle in the mud, eager to be on. Then across three large and inviting enclosures of permanent pasture separated by stout and not so inviting cut-and-laid fences each with a ditch on both sides. On to a gravelled driveway, and here the tracks disappear. We pull up and listen. A truck driver, standing on top of the cab of his truck, parked in a lay-by on the road, shouts to us.

"They're down in the bottom 'ere."

He points. We canter down to the road, cross it, and see hounds working slowly along the stream banks below us.

"I seen the fox," says the driver from his perch. "Went down along where they are now and up over the hill there to the Hartford road. I told Master but 'e just says 'Let 'em work it out for 'emselves'. Proper stew 'e's in. One of the cars was goin' too fast along the road 'ere an' nearly clobbered some of the hounds. Fair cursed 'im, Master did."

A leading hound turns up the hillside and begins to move on faster. She yips excitedly. The whole pack rushes to her and, confirming the line with a crash of music, storms on up the hill.

We trot down to the stream, scramble through the reeds and sedge to get over just in time to join behind the Field Master. On across the hill, over a stone wall and some rails over a wire fence and we come to the Hartford road; to find it jammed solid for a quarter of a mile with the cars of hunt followers. The hounds are rushing distractedly in and out of the cars and along the hedgerows, and the Master is in a fulminating fury.

"They say he's over the road, George," the Master fumes, "Over the roofs of the bloody cars, I suppose. Can't think how else he could have got across. I'll take hounds over. You keep the field this side. If we can't pick him up I'll try back here."

"Right," says the Field Master. He rides alongside the hedge, stands up in his stirrup-irons and glares down the line of car followers. The ice saw grates more stridently this time.

"Will you all please switch those damned engines off and keep quiet. We're trying to hunt a fox, not run a ruddy motor rally."

This rebuke provokes some huffing and puffing among the occupants of the cars, but they know they have offended and those who have not already switched off hasten shamefacedly to do so.

The Field Master turns to the field.

"Please keep bunched together in the middle of this field. If he hasn't crossed the road we don't want to get over his line this side. Let's give the hounds a chance."

The field huddle together. One or two dismount to check girths and I take the opportunity to level up my stirrup leathers.

The Master circles hounds in a wide cast round the ploughed field across the road, but there is obviously nothing there. He brings them back through the cars. His anger has given way to despondent resignation.

"I'll try round the hedgerow," he calls to the Field Master, "But we're a long way behind him now I'm afraid."

The bitches close to the line of the roadside hedge and work along it down to the corner. The Master trots on an inside circle behind them, cheering them on quietly,

"Yeeerrt, me girls. Yeerrt, me beauties. Try find 'im."

The hounds, steadied by his calm encouraging tone, get their

heads down and really work for the line. In the corner they turn
from the road and begin to push through the rough growth on
the double which lines the bottom end of the pasture. Suddenly
sterns begin to wave faster. There's a whimper and the lead
hounds, closing into a tight bunch swerve away from the bank
towards where the field is grouped. One hound speaks and then
the rest of the bunch, but a little uncertainly.

"Ware heel," the Master's roar echoes across to us. "Ware
heel, Dulcimer,—Charity, ware heel!"

Tom streaks across to head them off. The crack of his lash
under their noses brings them up short and they swing off either
way, their heads up. The Master canters over to the bank,
pulling his horn from between his top buttons. Before he can get
it to his mouth a long screeching holloa turns all eyes to a
solitary figure waving from the top of a haystack on the skyline.

The Master doubles his horn. Abruptly the tail hounds, still
running the line of the bank, all speak together and hurl themselves scrabbling through the thorn hedge, up and over its steep
side.

The Master's old chestnut hops neatly on and off the bank.
Tom's big horse flies the lot in an enormous leap. Now, riding
alongside the Field Master, it is my turn.

The mare rises at it, checks on the bank top, catches a toe
under a stump, begins to pitch, then flings herself forward out
over the ditch. She lands with her nose between her forefeet and
her hind legs slip back into the ditch. I am up her neck with my
hat over my eyes and my chin between her ears. Her off forefoot
flails, catching me on the point of my right knee and knocking
me back into the saddle. She gives a tremendous, grunting heave
and we're up, mud all over the front of her face and chest but no
cuts anywhere that I can see from under my now corrugated
hatbrim. My right leg is numb from the knee down.

She breaks at once into a canter and there are a few agonising
seconds until I regain my stirrup-irons. I have to lift my right

foot into the iron with the crook of my whip. The leg bears my weight when I stand up so I suppose it isn't broken.

A loose pony comes past me. It has no bridle, but in any case I am in no state to catch it and the next fence is on us almost at once. The pony checks at the fence and swings straight across in front of me. It is too late to stop. I can do nothing to help and the mare takes charge. Taking off further out from the fence than I would ever think possible she clears the pony's quarters and the fence together. I am too frightened even to swear at the pony. She lands cleanly well out into the next field and I feel a lot better.

This is plough and we pick a wide furrow and, mud flying, canter on down it to an old crumbling bank topped by a thin straggle of thorn. I sense rather than see the tangle of old wire round the dead stumps, but getting close to the bank, the mare pops easily over it off her hocks and I feel better still.

Before us the ground drops away into a narrow valley. Across it—glorious sight and sound—the whole pack is clamouring through the gorse climbing the steep, whale-back of Lytton Down. But now the butterflies flutter in the bravest of stomachs, for between the field and the hounds yawns the gloomy chasm of the Lytton Brook.

I have sometimes been asked by non-foxhunting friends why foxhunters will jump obstacles like the Lytton Brook, and my answer is always because—like Mount Everest—it's there; though possibly more people are prepared to jump the Lytton Brook. Anyway if you don't jump the Brook now the only alternative way to hounds is by the bridge in Lytton village, a mile down stream.

The water of the Lytton Brook is only ten feet across. But the banks crumble horribly for six steep and sombre feet down to the green weed twining slowly in the sluggish black depths. You need to take off well back and land well on from the banks; and you need to know you have to.

Fortunately the mare knows. I know she knows but it doesn't help much. Breathless with apprehension, I sit down but don't dare to push too hard for fear of unsettling her. My fears are groundless. Quickening for the last few strides she really stretches out for the far bank and goes over like a bird. I feel wonderful.

A few get over before and after me, and as we climb the side of Lytton Down, the strident shouts of the would-be brave and the resounding splashes of the luckless proclaim a damp, dramatic reduction of the field.

On up a short slope, over a stile in the wire fence at the top, and then our stride slows to the long climb across the down side along the narrow chalk cattle paths through the gorse.

As we come over the shoulder of the down, breathless, we slow to a walk, the horses stretching their heads down and snorting, their sides heaving.

Hounds have checked in a herd of cattle, which now huddle together, swinging lowered heads and snorting at any hounds near them. The bitches cast themselves all across the wide expanse of the close-cropped pasture, and the Master sits quiet, letting them work it out.

A county council dust cart crawls noisily over the crest from the opposite way and rumbles to a halt by the roadside across the field from us. The driver opens his door and leans out.

"I seen a fox down into the quarry back along. Goin' pretty slow, 'e were. Reckon 'e could be your'n."

The Master waves his whip in thanks, whistles to the hounds and sets off for the first of the hunt rails over the wire fences separating the big pastures on the downside. The dustcart driver slams his door, grinds into gear and trundling about, his engine roaring, disappears back down to the quarry in the hope of seeing a bit of sport. Some dust bins are going to be emptied late today.

Clear of the cattle foil the bitches are quick to pick up the line again and surge forward to the head of the path leading down the lip of the quarry. They disappear into its depths, overgrown with a tangle of bramble, gorse and elder.

Near the top of the path we hear them speaking with a deeper, sullen tone as they mark their fox to ground in the quarry bottom. We find them clustered round a hole scratched under the edge of a great slab of rock fallen from the quarry side.

"Hell's bells," says the Master, "We'll never get him out of that. This place is a damned labyrinth. There's thousands of holes like that and they all join up. We never can stop them all."

He gets slowly down off the chestnut, walks over and peers into the hole. Then he makes the quarry re-echo with the long notes of "To ground" and the bitches accompany him in an angry chorus.

We move out of the quarry on to the road. The dustcart driver leans out of the window of his cab. He sucks his lower lip and shakes his head sympathetically.

"Need some bloody dynamite to shift 'im, you would. Hope 'e give you a good run?"

The Master grins.

"He did. He doesn't owe us anything. Thank you for your help."

"Pleasure, sir," the driver answers, "Anytime. Me and my mates always likes a good 'unt." He nods to the first whipper-in, "I'll see yer, Tom," and letting his clutch in with a thump and a rasp of tyres he roars back up the hill.

"All on, sir," says Tom, and, Ben leading, the pack moves off in the wake of the dustcart.

The remnants of the field close in behind the hounds and I trot up the hill beside Tom. The dust from the truck hangs in the air and my throat feels dry as the barren rocks of Aden. I take out my flask and offer it to Tom. He takes a long pull and hands it back with a gusty sigh.

"Cor, that 'elps a bloke live through the day, sir." He looks around at the field, thirty strong that rode out five score. "Got thinned out a bit, ain't we? Never mind, they always says the more grief at the opening meet the less you'll 'ave in the season."

One Christmas Eve

OF ALL MEETS the one on Christmas Eve is my favourite. For me it has a special atmosphere of its own; a sort of cheerful expectancy remaining unaffected by even the dullest sort of day. Not that I can ever remember having a dull day's hunting on any Christmas Eve. We don't meet at any particular place as we do for the Opening Meet or the Boxing Day or Hunt Ball meets, and I particularly recall one Christmas Eve when we met at the "Three Horseshoes" in Compton Magna.

Compton Magna has seven more houses than Compton Parva; which has nine and a church. Compton Magna church was burned down by 'the Papist sodgers' in 1685 during the Monmouth rebellion, and as the "Three Horseshoes" dates from around then, one can only suppose that the stone from the ruined church served to build the pub. Since then the villagers of Compton Magna have walked the mile to Compton Parva church for refreshment of the spirit, whilst those of Compton Parva walk the mile to the Three Horseshoes to seek refreshment of the flesh.

Compton Magna is within easy hacking distance at the bottom of our hill. Riding down the quiet road on this Christmas Eve morning I was confronted at one of the many bends by a large roman-nosed chestnut horse. It was turning a slow circle on its forehand alternately lifting each hindleg in the unnervingly speculative manner affected by only the most efficient kickers. All I could see of the rider was the wide white expanse of breeches covering his southern extremities, and the backs of a pair of gleaming mahogany-topped boots. The remainder was under the horse apparently wrestling with the girth.

"Hold still, you goddam son of a bitch!"

Having the honour of the acquaintance of two American officers attached to my Regiment in Germany, I was familiar with this form of address and offered my assistance. Recognising the horse as one belonging to my brother-in-law, I grasped the bridle and adjured it to behave, employing the references to its doubtful antecedency he customarily uses. This has an invariably sobering effect on any of my brother-in-law's horses. The American and I were soon on our way.

He was a Virginian, a keen fox-hunter and on business in England. We are fortunate to have a few such visitors, and it seemed to us both especially appropriate that he should be hunting with English hounds over Beckford's own country on this particular day. That evening he was to fly back to the United States to spend Christmas in his own home; but he was determined to enjoy a day's fox-hunting in England before doing so.

The inn-keeper of the "Three Horseshoes" is, like every inn-keeper round here, a keen supporter of the Hunt. English law permits innkeepers to extend private hospitality at any hour of the day and the crowd outside the "Horseshoe" was taking full advantage of the privilege. I introduced my American acquaintance to the Master and Field Master and we both accepted a portion of the "Horseshoes" stock from the hands of the police patrol driver, who is also the inn-keeper's nephew.

We moved off through the usual Christmas Eve throng of riders, foot-followers and cars to the first draw. This was a four-acre field of winter cabbage. The crop, wilting and yellowed in places, had not done well and had been partially cleared. There were sizeable gaps in the cover it afforded. As we approached it Ben, the second whip, voiced the thoughts of all on the chances of finding a fox in it.

"Old Mrs. Thomas says that chicken-stealer she'm been moanin' about lies up 'ere. I reckon she'm daft or it is. 'oo'd lie up in this ole load o' rubbish?"

The master obviously agreed. Halting the field, he put hounds straight in from the gate, the two whips skirting the crop on either side.

Astonishment awaited him. Hounds had covered no more than a few yards when there was a positive explosion of foxes. Six—no less—broke at every angle; one of them right through the whole pack and the crowd of foot-followers standing in the gateway. Utter confusion followed. Everyone shouted, cars hooted, hounds owned all six lines at once and the Master, too amused to be angry, was laughing too much to blow his horn.

Order was partially restored by the whips who, not knowing which line the Master wanted, managed with the help of some of the foot-followers to stop all hounds except for two sections of the pack which disappeared in diametrically opposite directions, each after its own fox.

The Master recovered quickly. To the first whip—

"Tom, get on with those hounds on your side. You've got about eight couple. Get him if you can and then try to get back to me. Have someone to go with you, I'll need Ben with me."

Through the whole pack and the crowd of foot-followers

And to the Field Master—

"George, the field had better come with me."

Off he went on the other line with what hounds he had left.

Tom, baulked by the wire on his side of the cabbages, came clattering back through the gate. Fire was in his eye. Here was a good fox, eight couple of hard-driving dog hounds and no field to worry about. What more could any man ask? He called to me as he came out on to the road—

"Come and give us a hand, Colonel, will yer?"

"You'd better come too," I said to the Virginian, "This should be fun."

The three of us turned into the next field and before us lay at that moment the best view in Europe. A stout hedge and ditch confronted us. On its far side, halfway across the field, the eight couple of hounds, packed under the proverbial table-cloth, were screaming along in view of their fox, just slipping through the fence in front of them. Over and beyond stretched the green permanent pasture of the Tarrant Vale, intersected by serried ranks of hedge, ditch and bank all the ten miles as far as the main Shaston to Halesbury road. We set sail.

He was a straight-necked fox and with hounds running in view he wasted no time. We came up with hounds after twenty minutes of glorious, breathless pursuit. They had checked among some cattle. A high wire-infested bullfinch separated us from them and Tom swung off his horse at the gate in the corner by the road. A post office van screeched to a halt on the road beside him and the driver leapt out.

"Leave t' gate, Tom, I'll look to 'un. You get on wi' 'ounds. I see'd this ole fox into yon field from top th' 'ill there an' 'er 'ant come out. 'er's by there somewheres."

The cattle were bunched into a corner of the field, staring into the hedge.

Tom climbed aboard.

"They got 'un pinned up there, Colonel. I'll try and get 'ounds to 'un."

We rode slowly towards the cattle. Some hounds came to us and Tom called to them quietly.

"Yeerrt, me lads, yeerrt, me beauties. Look at old Warrior, Colonel, workin' the heel line to see where they went wrong. Good lad, Warrior, try find 'im."

Back at the bullfinch Warrior swung from the heel line up the hedge side. Suddenly he spoke, deep-toned, decisively. The hounds round Tom's heels raced to him. Up in the corner the lead bullock lurched a few paces forward, head down, snorting. Almost from under his nose a red-brown shape broke and swerved out into the mid-field. Too late. Before he had gone fifty yards Warrior was on him, and, taking him across the back, killed him cleanly.

Tom was off in a flash and into the snarling, heaving scramble. He took off the mask and brush and tossed the carcass to the hounds with a tremendous—

"Who-whoop—worry, worry, worry!"

He tied the mask to his saddle, then walked to where the Virginian stood, still breathless, beside his now thoroughly subdued and steaming chestnut. Gravely taking off his cap he held out the brush—

"I knowed Master 'ud like for you to have this, sir."

We came out again on to the road and the postman pulled the gate to behind us. Tom called to him—

"Thank 'ee, Harry. Right smart of you, that was. You'll be 'untin' 'ounds yerself next, lad. Happy Christmas to yer!"

On our way to rejoin the others we passed the cabbage field where we had found. A stout, old, gray-haired lady sat in a Landrover by the gate.

"Hello there, then, Mrs. Thomas" cried Tom, "We killed one o' your chicken worriers, ma'am."

D

"I should hope you did too, Tom Scarlett. They were having their Christmas dinner off five of my best pullets in there—all five taken last night, they were."

The Virginian removed his silk hat and bowed from his saddle.

"Ma'am," he said "Permit me to offer you my deepest sympathy in your loss. But I surely hope no one shakes up my Christmas dinner the way we did those foxes'! A very happy Christmas to you."

See Amid The Winter Snow

"You're going to get a wet shirt to-day," said my wife cheer-fully.

The wind rattled grey drifts of sleet against the windows and bent the tops of the fir trees along the road. We had been glad to have the wind at first. Coming from the southwest it had thawed out the frost which had stopped us hunting for the first week of the new year. But later it had brought the snow, which had now begun to lie.

"It's a Pony Club meet," I said. "Master asked me to help. Otherwise I'd be happy to stay home."

My wife laughed.

"You're just a fair weather fox-hunter. But I do hope you find quickly and get moving. It will be miserable for the children standing around in this rain."

The drive of the house where we met was a shambles of ponies, parents and children of all ages and degrees of sophistication. From the small, square, female hippo-maniac—all bulges, freckles and spectacles, with the ends of her plaits secured with binder twine, to the Lucy Glitters of the future, svelte, glossy, elegant and poised. As always, the ponies bore a marked resemblance to their riders. The few grown-ups, invited by the Master to assist with gate-shutting, pony-catching, restraint of the over-eager, encouragement of the fearful and first aid for the fallen, huddled defensively together. The uninformed onlooker might be forgiven for wondering who was in charge of whom.

We drew the wood behind the house blank and moved on quickly to Farley Bushes, a plantation of beeches and hazels, usually a sure find. Coat collars up and hat brims dripping, the field waited patiently whilst hounds worked through the covert. Again a blank, and the Master's horn sounded a little mournful as he called hounds out.

He halted by the field.

"Sorry things are a bit slow," he said, smiling cheerfully. "We had a good fox out of there three weeks ago. There are signs of a couple more of them in there now, but they're not at home to-day."

Looking round the circle of expectant faces he met the adoring, blue-eyed gaze of a small, plump girl on a small, plump pony. The small girl's blond plaits and the pony's blond mane were both secured with bright red ribbon, and they shared the same solemn expression.

"We'll try that kale field behind your house next, Susan. D'you think your father has got a fox for us there?"

The small girl turned the colour of her hair ribbon, too overcome to answer.

Clattering in a well-ordered cavalcade through the farmyard, the field waited fetlock-deep in the chalky clay beside the kale.

Up the hill they streamed

The wind had become colder and the sleet had turned to snow. Above us the stark skyline of the down appeared only fleetingly through the grey, driving flurries. The only sound apart from the wind was the bustling of the hounds through the sodden kale. Discomfort and inaction began to breed depression and boredom in the less hardy.

A hound spoke, and another, but their tone was uncertain and the surge of excitement subsided when none of the rest of the pack owned the line.

The Master turned toward the gate.

"Bring 'em on, Tom," he called. He raised his horn to call hounds but suddenly drew rein, the horn still silent at his lips. Two hounds had broken out through the hedge and were working towards a big patch of gorse on the hillside. The second whip began to rate them and, clearing the hedge, cantered up the hill in pursuit.

"Leave them alone, Ben," shouted the Master. "Old Warden there isn't one for riot."

The couple of hounds pushed into the lower edge of the gorse and at once gave vehement tongue. The snow cleared just at that moment and, from the top end of the gorse, a great, dark red dog fox, his black brush marked with a distinctive swatch of white, loped effortlessly up the hill into the wood which crested the down.

"Whoooooi!" Ben's tremendous long-drawn holloa brought the rest of the pack streaming out of the kale and up the hill, urged on by the Master's horn.

The excitement among the field was at once at fever pitch. Up the hill they streamed behind the Field Master, cold and discomfort forgotten. Waiting at the back to help the weaker over the hedge and up the hill, I reckoned that would be the last I should see of hounds that day and cursed my luck. This fox looked like a 'traveller' come to mate with the vixen living in an earth in the gorse out of which we had just pushed him. Gallant fellow that he was, he had drawn hounds away from his mate and would now probably head straight for his own home, wherever that might be—and it could be miles off. If I was right we could be in for a hunt to be remembered.

But it was not to be as easy as that. Arriving at the edge of the wood with an entourage of puffing ponies, the riders as breathless as their steeds, we met the Master trotting disconsolately down a ride towards us accompanied by only half the dog-hounds.

"Old Benson has got his sheep folded under the windbreak there. 'Course that cunning devil went straight to them. Never seen him before—must be a traveller. Hounds split up. Half of them have gone on through the wood and I've sent Tom on after them. Ben should be round here somewhere. I sent him to keep an eye on that top corner. You seen him?"

"No, Master. Do you want me to find him?"

"No, don't worry. Might as well go myself. If that fox is a traveller he'll want the easy way home, and wherever he wants to go that's along the top of the down here. Of course he may still want to hang around his girl friend."

Just at that moment another ear-splitting holloa echoed through the wood. Hounds' heads came up on the instant and for a second they froze, then, as the holloa rang through the leafless trees again, as one they raced, grimly silent, towards the top corner of the wood.

"Good lad, Ben!" said the Master and cantered after them.

"Come on, boys and girls," I said, "Now we've got a hunt."

But, of course, they were already away ahead of me.

He was a traveller all right, and I was happy for the children's sake that he did travel the crest of the hill. From that wood the downs swing round in a great curve to the southwest, and the droveway along which men have driven cattle for over two thousand years runs it's rutted path along the whole length. The down sides are in most places too steep to plough, and, under its covering of snow, the downland turf gave a firm footing. The children either careered along the droveway or, more intrepid, launched themselves recklessly over the rails dividing the fields beside it. Anyway they all got there in the end—and a long way it was.

Past Elksham and Fenton. Over the Blandbury road. Across the ancient camp on Tod Hill, where once the bored Roman sentries must have looked down from their earth and timber stockade at the green river valley below and longed for the hills and valleys of their home. Over Ledbury Beacon, where the villagers had stood by their blazing signal fire to watch the mighty Armada of Spain sail majestically up the Channel to ruin and defeat. And on, nine miles as hounds ran, to where they marked him to ground in the disused quarry above Stourmouth, the little port where some of the English ships had put in to patch their hulls and sails before hastening out again to harry King Philip's lumbering, towering galleons.

We heard the long, sad notes of "Gone to Ground" ahead of us, and when we came up with hounds the Master was on his feet amongst them and they were singing the mortified, heart-rending chorus that good, hard-driving dog-hounds will always sing when they have run their fox to ground. He turned away from the earth and climbed back, a little stiffly, on to his big bay.

"Come on, my lads, leave him. He's given us our money's worth. Leave him."

As the daylight faded we made our way down to the valley road where the Master halted hounds beside the "Stourmont Arms." He looked round the throng of weary, but beatifically happy children, and took off his cap.

"Well done all of you. I'm very proud of you. It was a good long hunt, wasn't it? But it was fun. I didn't want to dig him out, he'd given us too good a run. Anyway, we're in the Stourton Vale country here and you mustn't go digging out other people's foxes—especially their good ones. Now we'll all have a good, hot drink and I'll call all your homes and tell them you're all right. Then we'll go home together."

We started for home in a close-packed column, with Tom and Ben in front leading hounds. It was dark now and the wind had dropped to silence. The clouds had broken and a full moon turned the snow covered hills into ivory, fairy tale mountains. The lights of the villages winked at us through the still, clear air. The steam from our horses hung above us in a silver tinselled cloud. The thud of their hooves in the snow and the creak of saddlery was the only sound.

Someone said—

"Why don't we sing a song. It'll help pass the time."

And so they began singing the old children's songs and carols that I remembered learning. They didn't sing very tunefully, it's true, and not all the words were right, but nobody minded.

Then there was, for no reason that I recall, a long silence. The moon seemed to shine more clearly, the snow gleamed whiter on the quiet hills, the lights of the houses glimmered more welcomingly, the frost fire glittered and glistened on the roofs and the valley lay more silently serene and lovely than ever I remembered it. And then a single child's voice began, pure and true—

"See amid the winter snow,
Born for us on earth below—"

Suddenly, I felt tears in my eyes—and not from the cold. Sentimental? Unashamedly. An incongruous association? If you like. Just then it didn't seem to matter.

I've always liked to help at children's meets since then.

Conflict of Loyalties

HOUNDS HAD moved off. The meet was deserted except for the empty horseboxes and a bent rustic ancient enveloped in a very large, very old, Army greatcoat and whiskers. I pulled into the verge and started to get the mare out.

"Ben gorn twanty minute a'more," came a croak behind me. The ancient now stood poised above me on the bank, a fair reincarnation of Edgar Allan Poe's favourite bird. I made no reply, straining to get the tang of the buckle into the next hole of the girth and only succeeding in getting it into my thumb. At last, dripping sweat and blood, I was aboard.

I was a stranger to this hunt. "Where will they be now?" I asked the whiskers.

"Twanty minute a'more," came the funereal reply, "More'n twanty minutes gorn."

44

"Where will they be now?" I repeated in my best parade ground voice. It got through.

The whiskers waggled animatedly. "Rackon'll be in thic lil' ole wood abun Eddlesdun."

I consulted my map and found Eddlestone. It was surrounded with "lil' ole woods." Thinking it wiser to leave the decision on which of them was "abun" it until I got there, I thanked and took leave of my ancient counsellor.

I trotted fast to Eddlestone to find it, too, deserted. I pulled up and listened. Not a sound. I clattered on through the village down towards the river, high beech woods on my right, water-meadows on my left stretching down to the withy beds marking the line of the bank.

Through the clacking of the mare's hooves I heard a squeaking and rattling behind me. I turned in the saddle and saw a boy on a bicycle, feet on cross-bar and chin on knees, following me down the slope at an unsteady wobble. I waved him to stop and his brakes protested loudly, apparently without effect, for he found it necessary to drop both feet to the road and drag them along the gravelled surface. By this time he was well past me, continuing slowly downhill, squeaking, scraping, rattling and wobbling even more dangerously as he craned round to stare at me.

"Where are hounds?" I called.

"Wotcher say?"

"Have you seen hounds?"

"Wot?"

"Have hounds been here?"

The boy's gaze shifted past me and glazed. For a moment I thought he would be over the bank and into the water meadow. Then his head went round and down on to his handle-bars, his feet to the pedals, and away he flew. I turned and saw the Master coming out through a hunt wicket at the side of the wood. No Geiger counter was needed to detect the nucleonic

fury radiating silently from him. Even the beeches seemed to
shrivel at his approach.

"Do you mind making a little less noise?" he hissed. "There's
never any——scent in these——woods. It's hard enough for my
poor little bitches without you getting their heads up screeching
and stamping and shouting with your——friend."

At this point "my——friend" slithered out of sight round the
corner with a final screech and wobble of his blue-jeaned behind. My apologies for being late and a nuisance were received
with a grunt and the glare subsided.

"If you want to be useful for a change you might get down
to that corner. There's just a chance that one might try to slip
across to the withy beds. We'll be back through this gate if we
don't find, so you won't miss us."

The Master turned back into the wood and I trotted down the
verge to the corner, wondering which of the gods I had offended
to earn this morning's chapter of accidents. I was so wrapped up
in my own thoughts and the examination of my thumb, now cold
and throbbing, that when the mare stopped dead at the corner
and snorted, I lurched forward on to her neck knocking my hat
over my eyes. Pushing my hat back, I stared between the mare's
ears straight into the eyes of a fox—young, spindly, rough-
coated, obviously the runt of a late litter.

Fox's faces are very expressive. When met out of season they
vary from the "What the hell are you doing trespassing in my
woods" air, to the courteous—"Ah, good morning, lovely day
isn't it? Well, I must be getting along now." In season one sees
anything from the gently vexed "Oh Lord, another of the——
oafs," of the fox you have just headed, to the haughty disdain
of "Out of my way, peasants," on the face of the fox who con-
temptuously canters through the entire field waiting at the covert
side. But now, for the first time in my life, I saw fear on the
face of a fox, though hounds were not hunting him and the
woods behind him were still.

I turned and saw the master

We stared at each other for about half a minute and the only thought in my head was "Poor little brute, you could do with a good meal and a brush." Then, as I eased back into the saddle, he ducked his head and scrambled down the bank, along the ditch, through a drain under the road and across the water-meadows into the withy beds, all with the awkward clumsiness of an overgrown puppy.

Instinctively my hand lifted for the holloa, but as I watched him disappear into the reeds the pity of his fear and clumsiness took the voice out of me. How could I put these noted hounds and their equally noted huntsman on to his poor young back? My hand fell back to the saddle.

The next ten minutes passed in a schizophrenic frenzy. I assured myself that the cub could not have given them a run and the going was bad along the river. Excuses were useless. I was an unpunctual, ill-mannered cadger, unable to redeem my senti-mental self by putting my hosts on to their first run of the day from a notoriously bad-scenting draw. The only honourable thing left to do was to pay my cap and then slink away. But how I hoped they would find another fox in that wood; and, of course, they did not.

The hunt came down to the wicket and I rode to meet them. The latch clicked and the huntsman came through, his hounds pouring over the rails beside him. Seeing a stranger he called cheerily to me, "Sorry to disappoint you, Sir—there was some-thing there, but we could not make anything of it." I smirked feebly, and muttered something inane.

The secretary greeted me kindly as we jogged. "Always have to draw there first," he said, "More to show the flag than anything. There's foxes there all right, but even the bitches rarely hold to one and push him out. They were on to one to-day, but couldn't do anything with him. Sorry—just bad luck."

"Well, never mind," I murmured. "Perhaps he'll give you a good run another day."

I don't know how I'll answer for all this on Judgment Day
when the good Lord asks me to account for it. I'll have the holy
man of Assisi on my side, but what the devil is Saint Hubert
going to say?

Not Saint Andrew's Day

"HE'S BRED to race," said Geoffrey.

"Race what?" asked the Adjutant with a sneer.

"There's really no point in being rude about the poor horse," said Geoffrey.

"It's impossible to be rude about the brute," replied the Adjutant—like all Adjutants, a notoriously maladjusted, egocentric cynic.

"Anyway, Guy is going to ride him for me in the Adjacent Hunts' Maiden next Saturday week at Knighthill," said Geoffrey in the superior tone of one wishing to end a vulgar bicker.

The Adjutant gave me a long, cold stare. "Ah well," he said, "He's never been much use as a Signals Officer," and disappeared behind "Playboy."

The conversation had been about Geoffrey's horse, Saint Andrew—brown gelding, 16.2 h.h., aged, of uncertain breeding, though Geoffrey would never admit it; known to his friends as Andy. He was a fairish hunter with a will of his own and his own pace, at which, though not particularly fast, he would go on for ever. He was brave enough at his fences, but his methods of surmounting them were not always painless.

The results of these occasional uncertainties were obvious if one examined his legs. In fact, the Sergeant in charge of Regimental Stables used to say that he had never known a horse better named, because his legs were just like a Scotsman's—all ruddy knobs.

Everyone in the Regiment was ready to admit Andy's ability as a hunter, but enthusiasm for his prospects as a money-maker in point-to-points was lacking. So much so that when we came out of the paddock on the afternoon of the race he featured at fifteen to one on the bookies' boards, and despite this phenomenal price even his groom would hazard no more than four bob on the Tote, and was kind enough to tell me that he reckoned he had said goodbye to that.

His groom's estimation of his chances was endorsed by a large, red-faced lady in a bright blue, belted mackintosh and brown pork-pie hat, who stood with feet well apart at the rails by the first fence, scrutinising the runners as we went down under varying degrees of control to the start. She fixed each combination with a piercing stare and aired her opinion of it in a voice to match. A small man, who looked so miserable I could only suppose he had the misfortune to be married to her, stood beside her. He wore an enormous checked cloth cap pulled well down over his ears; presumably to preserve his hearing.

Having awarded a grudging "Well, that's all right" to the horse and rider ahead of me, she glared at Andy and me and without a moment's hesitation gave tongue:

"Oh, I don't like that one at all."

We got away to a good, even start and for the first mile Andy

E

seemed to be enjoying himself, though galloping and jumping rather faster than he was wont. Then we hit the first open ditch very hard, and after that I got the impression that he was beginning to think that all this haste was a bit unnecessary. To the best of my ability I encouraged him to continue with the rest of the field, but at the second open ditch he decided firmly that he had had enough of this vulgar rushing about and stopped.

I tried him at it again and yet again but he remained adamant, until a very military-looking gentleman in a shaggy bowler approached us at light infantry pace, swinging a shooting stick and commenting most rudely on Andy's ancestry, appearance and performance. Andy, apparently touched to the quick by these insults, hurled himself in his customary fearless style at the fence, but, in his haste to get out of range of the military gentleman's shooting stick, omitted to leave the ground. This is no way to surmount an open ditch.

There was a splintering noise as we hit the guard rail. Andy's front half disappeared into the fence and I continued flying solo straight and level at about four feet for a very long time. Then heaven and earth wheeled darkly about me and I heard two almighty thumps. One was Andy touching down and the other was me. The extraordinary thing was that though I was under the impression I had left him about half a mile back on the other side of the fence, when the dust settled I found we were gazing bemusedly into each other's eyes.

A very kind ambulance man helped me up. A cursory examination assured us that I was not lacking any essential part of my anatomy, and we turned to Andy, who continued to lie motionless at our feet, breathing heavily. The ambulance man was obviously no equine authority, but he did his best.

"Poor horsy," he said, "Poor old horsy then. Where's it hurt then, eh?" And he prodded Andy's ribs with a nervous finger.

I took the bridle and gave a tug at Andy's head. "Come on, Andy, get up, old boy."

One was Andy touching down and the other was me

Still motionless, Andy's look of pained reproach filled me with black thoughts of broken bones and other horrors. A paralysing indecision seized me.

We should have probably been there yet if it hadn't been for the military gentleman, who came whipping round the end of the fence with the air of one about to commit us all to the guardroom. On sight of him Andy gave a convulsive heave and then lay as still as a rabbit in front of a stoat, with much the same sort of expression.

"What's wrong, what's wrong, hey?" rapped the military gentleman, glaring at Andy as if he were a pair of dirty boots.

"Broke his poor old back, I reckon," said the ambulance man hopefully. The military gentleman rammed his shooting stick into the ground, bent down and rapidly pummelled and pulled Andy in all the right places. Then he jerked upright and glowered at the medical authority.

"Nonsense," he said shortly, and, seizing his shooting stick as if drawing a sabre, he gave Andy a sharp blow on his well-rounded hinder parts and in a voice of thunder roared: "Get up, you idle brute."

Andy, recognising the voice of real authority, immediately leapt upright and endeavoured to stand to attention, trampling in his confusion on the toes of the ambulance man, whose tender-hearted protestations on behalf of Andy's back turned smartly to profane comment on his size and clumsiness.

Now it was my turn. The steely eye was turned on me. "All right, boy?"

"Yes, sir. Oh yes, sir, thank you."

"Well, I'll put you up then. You might as well get round."

I thought Andy was going to faint, but he put the best face he could on it and submitted to my being put aboard again. Believe it or not, we did the final five fences in pretty fair style, though admittedly arriving a little late at the finish, I don't think Andy would have dared to refuse at any of them for fear of some

terrible reprimand echoing across at us from the area of the
second open ditch.

The lady in the blue mackintosh was there when we came in.
She favoured us with a glassy glare and turned to her spouse.

"What did I tell you?" she bellowed. He ventured no reply
and she didn't look as if she were expecting one. She probably
never does.

We never ran Andy again, and Geoffrey later confessed, in
strictest confidence, that he would never have considered running
him at all if his current girl friend hadn't admired Andy at some
lawn meet and asked Geoffrey in front of a lot of other gorgeous
giggling things if he was going to race him. What could poor
Geoffrey say? What indeed?

It later transpired that the silly bitch didn't know one end of
a horse from the other. However, she got her just deserts in the
end. She married the Adjutant.

APRIL

To Finish the Season

"To FINISH the season" the Hunting Appointments column had said and, on leave from Germany, it would be my only day that season. So, as we trotted up the road to the first cover, the Master was kind to me.

"Get up to the far corner of the wood, Guy, you know where I mean, overlooking the village. The old devil in here either breaks into that big pasture up there or down over the road to the river. We'll line the road down here or he'll have us into the floods in no time. Don't give him too much law if you see him or he'll turn down into that damned rubbish tip—all ruddy broken bottles and cans, not much good for the hounds' feet."

I trotted past him and up the track to the hunt wicket leading into the wood, where the huntsman sat quietly talking to his hounds, waiting the order to put in.

🏵

Looking up at the sound of my mare's feet he grinned cheerfully in recognition.

"Hello, sir, back on leave? Nice to see you out again. You
going to the top end? With this wind he'll be sure to break
there. Give us the tip as soon as you see him, will you, or the
beggar'll have us down in that rubbish dump—"

"I know," I said, "The Master told me. What if I head
him?"

"Head him? You won't head this one, sir. Like as not he'll
spit in your eye as he comes out. We been after him for three
years, this one. Regular old sport he is."

The warm, wet wind roared through the beeches as I rode
to the top of the wood. When I reached it I looked down at the
river winding through the sodden valley, swollen by the April
rains. It swirled and wreathed, steep-banked, round the corner
beneath the willows, then opened into a slowly shifting, ever
widening, steel grey flood, reaching further and further out over
the water meadows until it lapped at the bank of the valley road
which runs through the village.

The gate at the head of the ride was new, very big and very
black. The catch was equally new and very stiff, and the mare,
feeling her oats and the wind under her tail, was in no mood to
stand still and let me struggle with it. The mud under the gate
was above her fetlocks. I glanced down fondly at my softly
gleaming boots and spurs still unflecked by the chalky clay—and
looked for a gap in the hedge.

We humped over a ditch into the wood, and the mare bucked
at once as she landed, lunging sideways into some hazels which
switched stingingly across my face, nearly knocking my hat off.
I swore at her, banging her on the flank with my whip, and she
relaxed, snorting at my poor sense of humor. We found a gap in
the hedge over the steep, slippery, little bank, where a couple of
ancient tangled strands of wire waved in the wind like witches'
claws, and scrambled out.

On the field gate leading into the pasture sat three small boys, huddled like rooks on a branch. The middle one wore a very old, shiny hunt cap, tilted well forward over his eyes. He nudged the one nearest the latch who dropped to the ground and swung the gate open. I rode through and pulled alongside the hedge.

"Thank you," I said, "Seen the fox yet?"

Hunt cap, obviously the leader of the trio, shook his head.

"Takes 'is time, this 'un."

Somewhat abashed by such expert local knowledge, I sat silent and was rewarded a couple of minutes later by the sudden appearance on the top of the bank of a large dog fox. He was not a handsome specimen, his coat was dull and tatty, his brush thin and raggety and his muzzle very grey and very pointed. But his air of complete self-assurance made up for all this. He surveyed the empty fields before him rather as, I imagine, Wellington must have surveyed the field of Waterloo before the battle. The enemy hadn't got a hope.

With an effortless leap he was across the ditch and into a long, easy, unhurried lope. I holloaed. Most foxes I have holloaed away have dropped their heads and brushes and gone smartly into overdrive. Not this one. He stopped short, listened for a moment, then sat down, turned his head and, I swear it, grinned at me.

From the huntsman, down at the bottom of the woods, there was no answering horn, so he couldn't have heard my holloa. This the veteran Charles James obviously appreciated, for he sat in the middle of the field grinning at us for all the world as if he was saying,

"Go on, have another bash."

Before I could oblige him the situation was retrieved by Hunt Cap, who, hand to face, gave vent to a sound like a pig in extremis. His exertion earned the reply of the horn down the wood and a look of respect from Charlie, who, apparently satisfied that activity would no longer be wasted effort, got to his feet

But the hedge looked too inviting

in leisurely fashion, trotted to the far hedge, slipped through it and was gone.

I heard the hounds, urged on by the shrill, stirring staccato encouragement of the horn, racing up through the woods towards me. The rustle and patter of their feet on the beech leaves gave way to a glorious chorus as, one after the other, they opened on the line. Down over the bank they came in a leaping cascade. Heads low, clamouring like a peal of bells, they swept over the field before me like the wash of a flood tide. Shoving, straining and scrabbling they were through the far hedge and on; on with a lovely ringing cry; on—I was very much afeard—to the rubbish dump.

The huntsman came thudding up through the trees and out over the hedge and ditch in a great swinging leap.

"They're a couple of minutes behind him, Tom," I shouted.

"Ah, damme," he called back, "That's two too many for the old varlet. You'd best come with me, sir." And he was over the next hedge.

As I went to follow him Hunt Cap shook his head.

"You don't want to go worriting about down the hill there, sir. They'll lose im' for sure in the rubbish and 'e'll be back 'ome up 'ere agin 'fore long."

But the hedge looked too inviting.

True enough we lost him. Not in the rubbish dump, but among a clutter of chicken houses and shanties huddled along the hedge beside the valley road.

A breathless man, wheeling a bicycle, opened the gate for us on to the road.

" 'E's on Tom," he puffed, "Hounds not more'n a minute be'ind 'im. Gurt, big, black dog fox. I seen 'im round they chicken runs there a 'undred times. Mind you get 'un. Lovely big brush 'e's got."

Tom looked at me, grinning with fury, slapping his boot with his whip.

"Ah, damn 'im," he ground, "Damn 'im. The old varmint must've pushed this new feller out from under them chicken houses. I'll wager the artful old cuss is setting under there a-grinning at us now."

Judging from his performance at the covert side I had no doubts on the matter. But delay was pointless. Hounds were on and couldn't be stopped; and for our old grey friend another season was definitely finished.

MAY

The Summering of the Hunter

"WILL I BE glad to see the last of those horses for this season!" I suppose this remark is made at least once around the end of April by anyone who hunts regularly. The freedom of the hunting field has become frustratingly restricted by then. The winter wheat is coming up well, new seeds are in and the cattle are out. Farmers are busy and though the hunt is tolerated it is not really welcome. The majority of hunt supporters are busy too, training horses, attending point-to-points, digging gardens, looking out fishing rods and painting boats.

However, if you are one of these who agree with Mr. Jorrocks that any moment not spent fox-hunting is wasted, you can, in late April and early May, occasionally enjoy a pleasant day in the select company of the Master, huntsman, the whips and one or two other devotees, in a part of the country which is not usually hunted during the rest of the season, and, for that very reason, is certain to hold a fox.

But the time comes inevitably in every hunting stable for the horses' shoes to come off, and the daily routine of putting out by day and in by night to begin.

And what a moment that is, when with shoes off and no saddle on, the hunters are lead into the pasture for the first time.

"Are you ready?"

"No! Don't let him go yet, I can't undo this damn buckle."

"Quick—she's pulling my arms out."

"Get off my foot you ugly great brute! For heaven's sake hurry up with that buckle before this monster eats me."

And so on. Until finally, all buckles loosed, all head ropes off, away they go, heads in the air one moment, heels the next. Galloping, bucking, fly-jumping, kicking—all at top speed, squealing their heads off, whilst you stand by the gate wondering why their legs don't break. Suddenly one attempts what the Air Force calls a maximum rate turn; his feet fly away from under him and he lands flat on his side. Your heart stands still and you start to run towards the prostrate form. But before you get there he is on his feet, shaking himself and looking slightly foolish. He slouches off into the corner, a little stiffly, tail swinging. His whole rear end seems to say, a little sulkily, "I meant to do that—just to frighten you."

The others, ignoring the fallen, are rolling and rolling and rolling in the dust under the clump of beeches. Then they get up and, with heads down and feet well apart, shake the dust out of their coats. It looks a most satisfying performance. Imagine how luxuriously gratifying it must be to lie on your back in a nice scratchy sand patch and wriggle and roll until you have got rid of all your itches and stiffness. Of course, for it to be really stimulating you have to do it in the nude, so you need an uncritical lot of neighbours.

In the evening when you go to get them in, you face one

of two situations. Either it is warm and they don't want to be caught—and you are already late for a party—or, feeling the beginning of the frost reported on the wireless, they are standing in a woebegone, reproachful bunch by the field gate ready to trample all over you in order to get back to the comfort of their boxes.

I recall negotiating to buy a mare from a large brother officer about to get married and in need of cash. He told me that she didn't jump very well for him but perhaps it was his weight. I called at his regimental stables on a cold drizzly April day and observed, in passing, a nice looking mare standing untied in an open box, quietly eating what remained of her bedding. I found the groom and told him what I sought.

"Captain Whatmore's mare, sir? She's in the field out the back."

"Whose is that bay mare standing in the end box?"

"In the end box? That's not Captain Whatmore's . . . Blimey, it is! Ow'd she get there? I put her out a hour ago myself. First time she's been out since he finished hunting. Must've got the gate open."

We led the mare out to the field. The gate was still securely latched; a stout four-strand wire fence surrounded the paddock.

"Well, how the hell did you get out, you artful old bag?" the groom asked fondly. "Proper artful she is, this one, sir." I looked at the dried earth in the gateway.

"Looks as if she jumped the gate. See where she's landed out here? That gate is all of four foot six. Captain Whatmore said she didn't jump too well."

"Not with fourteen stone of Captain Whatmore on, she don't. No, sir."

We put the mare back in the field, latched the gate, walked back down the lane to the corner and waited. Sure enough, immediately we were out of her sight, the mare began to trot in a wide circle, then, turning towards the gate, broke into a slow

Galloping, bucking, fly-jumping, kicking—all at top speed

canter. She got the gate just right and sailed sweetly over it, checked and turned on landing in a beautifully balanced style and trotted straight back to us. Her face when she saw us waiting at the corner was quite a picture. I told the groom to leave her in and bought her that day. She obviously had a mind of her own and plenty of courage and determination. And she could jump.

Soon, of course, the novelty of being out alone, without the hindrance of some ham-fisted, top-heavy human to interfere and restrict, wears off. The horses begin moving slower. There is less squealing, kicking and biting, fewer sudden mad cavorts at breakneck pace round the field. Soon too, sooner than you had originally intended, comes the warm evening when you say—

"I think it's warm enough for them to stay out to-night, isn't it?"—and they are out for good.

Then conscience strikes when, two evenings later, leaving some evening function, you feel the bite of frost in the air. Arrived home, you rush anxiously down to the field gate and are slightly put out to find them happily munching away under the already thick foliage of the chestnut trees, or else clustered dozily in the lean-to by the water trough and obviously irritated by your clumsy disturbance. Tails swish, feet stamp, and they nuzzle one another and snort—blinking in the light of your torch—

"What on earth is the fool doing fussing around here this time of night?"

"The man's drunk, my dear, don't talk to him. Come away."

And off they lurch sleepily, snorting and blowing and giving the most ghastly hacking coughs just to scare you. You feel simultaneously a cad for having left them out and a fool for having doubted their ability to look after themselves. On this performance they have scored in the unceasing game of "One upmanship" which constantly enlivens one's association with the not-so-dumb beasts the Lord has entrusted to one's care.

Later you will watch with satisfaction as the flesh builds up over the ribs and behind the saddle. You will recall the sense of shame you felt when towards the end of March a tactless oaf— only out for the fourth time that season and mounted on some gross beast—had remarked that your horse was looking a little light; the implication being that you were either starving him or over-working him, probably both. He had certainly never lacked for oats though perhaps you had hunted him a bit hard. But anyway he loved his hunting and hadn't missed a day through unsoundness; and just look at the old black barrel now with his sleek fat sides, his tummy like a mare's in foal, his overlong doormat of a tail, and the thistle heads and mud he has collected rolling and rolling to scratch away the memory of the pressure of the saddle. Nobody could call him light now.

Now when you go to visit them on the long warm evenings you see them standing head down, unhurriedly pulling away at the turf, tails a-sweep, heads lifting occasionally to shake off the flies and snort out the dust and prickles. They eye you sleepily as you approach and stand four square chewing slowly and deliber- ately, or come in leisurely fashion towards you when you call, stopping every so often to swing their heads and nip at the flies teasing their withers and flanks. They are in no hurry and you had better not be either. Slovenly now in their eating they slobber over the tidbit you present them, leaving your hand slimy with the greenish froth of chewed grasses.

They look fat and contented and well and idle; and not much inclined to pick their own feet up to let you rasp them. You hope they will stay that way and not venture to explore a route out on to the main road; eat something that disagrees with them; get tied up inexplicably and bloodily in the fence; bite, kick or otherwise maim each other, or indulge in any of the other unpredictable stupidities by which horses out at grass occupy a little of their time and a lot of yours—usually at the most inconvenient hours.

F

Later still, the flies will begin to worry them, and the routine of bringing them in before breakfast and putting out again before supper begins until—good heavens!—they're cub-hunting tomorrow. You will have to keep the mare in to-night. The old devil will never let you catch her in the morning. And it seems only yesterday that you let them out.

The Puppy Show

EITHER IT'S held "by kind permission of—" in which case it's rather a slap-up affair. Everyone dresses reasonably smartly and gossips in an aura of shaven lawns, white tents, rings all meticulously squared and taped, cucumber sandwiches, tea-urns and calm decorum; with the puppies all securely fenced in neat, little hurdled enclosures behind the delphiniums.

Or else it's at the kennels. Then the ring is an uncertain circle enclosed by an old rope or a couple of lungeing reins; the 'tea' comes out of crates in the back of the Master's Landrover; the aura is enhanced by the rich, summer smell of the kennel drains mingled with a soupçon of disinfectant and that indescribable sour tang of boiling flesh; you can't hear yourself think for the noise the hounds are making, and the puppies trip you at every step.

Whichever way you hold it, it is the consummation—the omega—of the puppy walkers' year. Now is the day of judgment. Solomon, blue pin-striped and bowlered, is come in the persons of the Master of the Wheremore Vale and the kennel-huntsman of the Blankly, to decide which of the season's litters conform to their ideas on the type of hound needed to hunt this country. Not everyone is going to agree with their decisions, and don't think for a minute that the Master of the Wheremore Vale and the kennel-huntsman of the Blankly don't appreciate this. And don't think for a moment that they give a damn. A man who hunts hounds gets accustomed to holding strong opinions and having his own way. He also gets used to listening courteously and sympathetically to people who disagree with him—and continuing, courteously, to go his own way.

First, "by kind permission" let us enter the aura of decorum on the lawn of a stately home. Prompt on the stroke of three the judges stalk into the ring with the stiff jerky stride adopted by the modest and unassuming when suddenly promoted to centre stage, talking a little more than they are wont and laughing a little too heartily. The Master of the Wheremore Vale is easily identified; you have met him elsewhere. But until you look very closely you find it hard to identify that little man, his companion judge, in his heavy, square, blue suit and his bowler resting on his prominent ears, with the neat figure in pink coat and gleaming tops sitting on a big, black gelding amid his hounds, which was your only image to date of the kennel-huntsman of the Blankly.

Soon, under the direction of our own kennel-huntsman, the doghound puppies are herded into the immaculate ring. Spectators, leaning on the ring fence, point and comment with a suddenly acquired expertise. The judges turn slowly on their heels watching a particularly favoured hound, consult quietly with an occasional gesture and scribble furiously on their cards.

After a while a few hounds are pulled out of the scrum and

And now there he is, away out in front

sent to a corner to await closer inspection. Spectators who claim to have picked these very hounds themselves nod sagely in approval of the judges' choice and try not to look smug.

One large puppy slouches off to cock a leg on the corner post, stolidly ignoring the second whip's furious, incoherently muttered commands. This throws everything out, all the other hounds now taking time off in succession to sniff and add their contributions to the post. Affairs begin to get out of hand, until the second whip is stationed at the danger spot to urge hounds away and order reigns again. That is, until two of the unfavoured entries, bored with the whole affair, take sudden, violent exception to one another and have to be removed from the ring in a snarling, scrabbling tangle.

Inspired by this tumult, every canine within earshot outside the ring immediately shouts its head off and hurls itself to the full extent of its lead at any animal in sight. The loudest outcry comes from the enclosure where the bitch puppies are waiting for their debut. The first whip storms across to them uttering that peculiar grinding noise which invariably reduces hounds to abject repentance. As he approaches the clamour of the bitches subdues to whimpers and squeaks. They caper round the pen in clumsy leaps, they roll over and lie on their backs waving their outsize feet at him, they jump up awkwardly as he stands by the fencing. They drool and pant and slobber, their enormous, dark eyes mirrors of innocence.

"What me, sir? Making a noise, sir? Oh no, sir, not me, sir. It was those nasty, rude hunt terriers next door!"

The hunt terriers are all in a pen next to the bitch puppies. I have always liked the idea of bringing them to these shows; one sees them all too rarely to appreciate their sterling qualities. They, of course, haven't made a sound. Terriers save their breath for the fight. Now they sit, neatly erect, on their haunches, occasionally quivering all over and swearing horribly with that ominously muffled, guttural snarl, which, starting at the nondescript stump of a tail, forces its way up through the taut form and out under a lip, curled just enough at the corner to show their white teeth. Now and then one will get up, stretch, stalk stiff-legged and unhurriedly round the pen, pausing to glower in silent scorn at the neighbouring puppies, and return to sit, balanced, alert, impassively watching the world go by, completely self-confident and entirely self-possessed. If any dog is master of its fate and captain of its soul it is the hunt terrier.

Now they squat, immobile, staring the first whip squarely in the eye.

"Noise? Us? Listen. If you can't tell the difference between us and the row those gormless goofs next door make you oughtn't to be a whip. And anyway, what if we did kick up a din? D'you want to make something of it?"

The afternoon moves on in leisurely fashion until the class for couples of puppies, handled by those who had them at walk, is called. This is the highlight of the show and well worth watching. It is supposed to offer everyone present the opportunity to admire the excellent condition and admirable discipline of the puppies, when handled by those unselfish supporters of the hunt in whose care they have been since they were taken from their dams. Sometimes it does.

Usually the kennel-huntsman stands by you, gloomily muttering, sotto voce—

"What in hell have the Blocks been feeding poor little Rufus and Remedy there? Look like a couple of in-calf heifers (or alternatively—"a couple of perambulating hay racks.") Never should have let them have a couple."

Then, as Mrs. Block is towed past, panting, by her charges, he changes to full volume in a cheerful tone,—

"Remedy and Rufus look well, Mrs. Block, ma'am. You got 'em just right. I like to see plenty of flesh on a puppy," and, as she passes from earshot, sotto voce again, "But not so's he can't hardly waddle."

Or his alternative comment at full volume—

"I like to see a puppy looking clean and light like that," followed, back to sotto voce, by—"But not so's I can see right through the poor little devil."

But then, he says the same of every puppy, including the ones you walk for him.

Now Mrs. Block and her fellow puppy-walkers are in the ring trying to range themselves into some sort of order. The more experienced have secured both puppies into one hound couple and to it attached a single, chain-ended leash. The chain end prevents the puppies chewing straight through it, and the spare length provides the handler with an effective medium of encouragement to good behaviour. The inexperienced have each puppy on a separate leather lead. This way the handler is certain to suffer anything from a sprained wrist to actual dismemberment. It also ensures with equal infallibility that both hounds will get loose.

I have seen many such crises on many occasions, and even made a little money betting on who is going to require medical attention first and the order in which the puppies will escape.

The most memorable of such emergencies—and regrettably I hadn't had time to negotiate any wagers before disaster struck —was when a couple of what were obviously going to be hard driving bitches tripped their handler, dodged out of the ring and put up our large and insufferably pompous hostess's insufferably pompous Pekinese out from under her chair.

It was a hunt never to be forgotten. Off round the ring with a tremendous cry, more hounds joining them as they went; flat out into the tea tent, upending the inattentive and unagile; round under the tables,—bottles, glasses, cups and sandwiches bouncing and richocheting; through the legs then over the toppled, - prostrate and loudly protesting form of the tea urn lady; out under the tent wall—quite a check for hounds that was—some of them losing interest and rioting on to the sandwiches; in and out of the tent ropes with puppies knocking themselves silly or getting strangled in the guys, and back to ground under the chair of our now hysterical hostess.

But the bitches were not to be deprived of their quarry. Avoiding the onslaught of parasols, handbags, hats and a plate of rather dry seed cake, they pushed him out again for a last desperate burst, ventre-á-terre, under the thick box hedge—another check; up and over the rockery skidding round the swimming pool, under the box hedge again and into the immaculate rose garden where they lost him, the infuriated gardener repelling the leading hounds with the full power of his hose; not, unfortunately, before many of his more exotic specimens had suffered considerable defoliation.

But though we all contributed to the cost of the roses, and a new hair-piece for the tea-urn lady, we were never asked there again.

In comparison the atmosphere of the show when held in the kennels is refreshingly relaxed and unstarched, though the fastidious might complain of its redolence. The judges—possibly not attired de rigeur in these circumstances—stand, glass in hand, commenting a little less restrainedly; they have to in order to make themselves heard. For despite the kennel-huntsman's repeated injunction to all the older hounds to—

"Hold your noise, will you, or I'll be in there!"—he never has time to be, so bedlam is perpetual and a glorious noise it is.

On the other hand the organisation is probably better, since we are playing on home ground and don't have to worry about the chances of ruining the lawn or devastating the dahlias. The puppies are properly secured, the kennels supplying the right equipment. However, this doesn't stop an inadequately restrained leash taking you smartly behind the knees and prostrating you, a welcome target for the large and filthy feet of every puppy near enough to leap enthusiastically to your assistance, before you can rise sufficiently to beat them off.

The routine here is the same as in the plushier setting. But spectators are few, more conversant with the management of hounds, and none have been so unwise as to bring unwanted canine friends.

At the end, in whatever surroundings, those noble souls who have submitted themselves to the alarms, the crises, the infuriations and, let it be truthfully added, the several joys, of responsibility for a couple of hound puppies are properly and deservedly rewarded; some few by the prize for the best puppies shown that day, the most by a token of the Hunt's gratitude for their generous services.

But for anyone who has had puppies at walk the real reward comes when, at the meet, the entered, seasoned hound, recognising its former guardian, comes, stern waving, head high, pushing through the pack to greet him with a big grin and a slobbery salute.

And then to watch from horseback, car or on foot, how, when hounds check and spread wide casting themselves to find the line, the first to own it and put them all right is Warden. Warden, who stole four pounds of sausages and a ham off the kitchen table and the vet had to use a stomach pump on him. Warden, who got chased by cows into a farm midden and couldn't be let into the house for weeks. Warden, who was found by old Middleton's gamekeeper, stuck in the hatch of one of his pheasant rearing pens. Warden, for whom you spent too many cold, wet nights out on the down searching, worried sick that he had been run over or was stuck in a hole or in wire. And now there he is, away out in front, head down, driving on, showing them all the way. And to see him there and hear the huntsman's—

"Yooi Warden. Good lad Warden. Hark to Warden all of yer!"—is the most satisfying and fittest requital for all your care.

Horse Shows and Hunter Trials

I WOULD POINT OUT to anyone about to criticise the grouping of
horse shows and hunter trials under one title and under the same
month, that I am encouraged to unite them under one title by no
less an authority than the Lonsdale Library volume on "Fox-
hunting," and in one month by the fact that there are not
enough months for the purpose of doing justice, even in my
inadequate way, to all the events of the foxhunter's year. Both
being competitive events they are not unrelated. And having
competed optimistically and having been involved haphazardly
in the organisation of both, I assure you that they occasion the
same triumphs and disasters, the same jubilations and frustra-
tions, the same thrills and boredoms, and that the organisers—
whose names rarely appear in the front of the programme
among the patrons and the other nobs—usually end the day the

❀

same way in the same bar imbibing the same Lethean waters for the same purpose. So to discuss them in the same chapter seems to follow naturally.

Colonel V.D.S. Williams, MFH, writing in the Lonsdale Library's "Foxhunting," reminds us that—

"The primary object of all horseshows is to improve and encourage the breeding of horses on an economic basis."

And that—

"The primary object of all hunter trials is to discover the most valuable horse to go hunting on, conformation, manners and performance being combined."

These are excellent precepts, to be observed implicitly by those in authority on these occasions, and most especially by those guardians of the Holy Grail, the judges, upon whose decisions so much depends; often more than they care to imagine. Bearing these "primary objects" steadfastly in mind, the experienced judge will never forget the probability of the existence of the variety of secondary objects of these events. These secondary objects will rarely be obvious to many, being intensely personal to the competitors and their supporters, and directed towards furthering the sporting, social or financial standing of the individual competitor or supporter—usually all three at the same time—at the expense of everybody else. Frequently they will entail the most involved machinations before, during and—if the judge is known to be of infirm purpose—even after the event. If Colonel Williams' "primary objects" provide the judges with their guide and purpose, the secondary objects provide them with their personal interest and their laughs.

There are all manners and degrees of horse shows, some of which only remotely observe Colonel Williams' "primary objects," but which, nevertheless, provide amusement and entertainment for all associated with them and valuable competitive experience for the younger or novice entrants for whom they are intended.

The hunters they themselves would most prefer to ride

The biggest, though not always the best, are those run under the aegis of the annual Agricultural or County Shows. These are large, somewhat impersonal and crowded. The catalogue is beautifully produced, expensive, weighs a ton and is replete with glossy, coloured advertisements and photographs of the always distinguished and often portly patrons of the Show, alongside the equally distinguished and inevitably portly champions of the fat stock classes of previous years.

The large—often permanent—show ground is neatly planned and traversed by well laid out avenues, each lined by a variety of stands, stalls and booths at which you can purchase every imaginable agricultural aid, from a mammoth combine harvester for your thousand broad acres to a quarter-pound packet of super-energised, dehydrated, non-odorous, guaranteed organic fertiliser for your one window-box. You can buy a new car, a Hampshire Down ram or a genuine Mexican cactus. What has all this merchandise got to do with the foxhunter attending the Show in order to compete in the showing or jumping classes? Not much; except that whenever I do I somehow never end up with an impressively massive silver trophy or rainbow galaxy of rosettes and ribbons—but invariably with a clutter of barn cloches and a Himalayan cyclamen.

The showing and jumping classes at these big shows attract mainly the higher grade entry from the better known stables and stud farms and the foremost professional and amateur riders. Competition is keen and to win or be placed confers considerable distinction and reward.

In the big ring, the centre piece of the whole show, the stars of the show-jumping fraternity perform with practised ease and precision over a horrifying and kaleidoscopic conglomeration of unnatural obstacles. For the majority of the audience the riders and their horses are, until to-day, only television acquaintances. Now, thrillingly, they are in the flesh, surmounting impossible piles of polychromatic poles, incandescent red brick walls, improbable stiles, gargantuan garden seats and the most unrural rustic gates. Here and there, now and then, a pole or wooden brick from the wall will topple, almost apologetically, and from the resultant despairing lamentation of the audience you would have thought utter disaster had overwhelmed them to a man. Sometimes even a hitherto faultless performance suddenly terminates in a resounding crash of shattered timber; poles, flags, stands, bricks and flower-pots fly in gloriously colorful confusion, and the arena party scurry like rabbits to reconstruct the barricade. It's a wonderfully gay and exhilarating spectacle—especially when it isn't raining—and the biggest draw of the show.

At other times, or in other rings, the junior aspirants to international fame jump over other courses, less intimidating in dimension, showing identical, inexorable dedication. The spectators assembled at these ringsides are fewer in number than the audiences attendant on the championship classes, but, being largely composed of parents of the competitors, rival them in their intensity of emotional expression; ranging the gamut from hysterical hallelujahs of praise to profane intentions of infanticide.

But true dedication to the mystique of showing lies in the quiet, almost deserted ring, when the hunters and working hunters are paraded for the judges. To the many unacquainted with the practice, the showing of the horse is a mechanical, plodding occupation, bereft of the emotion and excitement of the jumping ring. But this is where the knives are really out. This is where emotional involvement in a performance can be observed at its best—and sometimes at its unbest.

Showing a horse is something of a science, something of a technique, and something of a coldblooded, ruthless, ride-over-'em-roughshod operation of war. The true showing owner or trainer of show horses of any sort on arriving at the show ground makes an immediate, military-style appreciation of the weather, the going, the size of the ring, the known likes and dislikes of the presiding judges, the probable performance of the horse, the probable performance of the rider, the number, identities and probable performances of the other competitors together with their known characteristics and past behaviour patterns in the show ring; from all these factors forms his, or her, plan of attack and issues orders accordingly. This mental process is inbred, automatic, far faster in operation and a damn sight more accurate than any computer, depending, of course, on the experience of the owner. A showing owner computing is an impressive sight, but I advise against addressing any remark to one so engaged. If you dare to do so and are fortunate you may find yourself merely ignored; unfortunate, and you will certainly be headless.

By now you will have gathered that, though a fervent admirer —even a student—of the genus horse shower, I lack the dedication and, more important, the basic desire to belong to this select community. I have been connected with, and occasionally related to, some of its devotees, and have appeared in the ring tugging—or being carted by—hunters in hand or under saddle. I have invariably been dumbfounded by the total inability of the judges to appreciate the patently superior conformation of my mount, and, more incomprehensible yet, their failure to remark the superlative skill with which I have shown the horse. Inevitably, it seems, I have been numbered amongst 'the excused.' It's a souring experience after a time.

But if you think you have witnessed the ultimate in dedication, devotion and intensity of emotional involvement in your observation of the showers of hunters, wait until you examine the show pony cult. Here is a monotheistic sect more furious in its fervour than any gaggle of Vestal Virgins. Brushed, be-ribboned, polished, combed and plaited, the impeccable ponies with their immaculate riders circle and circle with meticulous precision the bravest men and women—some say the most foolhardy

—in creation, the judges. Outside the ring glowering cohorts of mothers, like the hymnal hosts of Midian, "prowl and prowl around"; with very much the same purpose in mind as the Midian host.

> *Men have many faults,*
> *Poor women have but two,*
> *There's nothing good they say*
> *And nothing right they do.*

The author of this couplet has chosen to remain anonymous. I suspect he was regretting having exposed himself to the vengeance of the disappointed majority of the Midian host.

Ballet and stage mothers, mothers of child prodigies and mère-disant geniuses are all horrendous in their thwarted wrath. But the Furies themselves could not rival the fulminating ferocity of the Pony Club mother whose child has been put down. Watch her stalk the unsuspecting judge as he wanders incautiously from the sanctuary of the ring. Hear her clarion cry ring out, ominous in its exaggerated courtesy—

"Would you be so very kind as to explain exactly why you put my child's pony down?"

The judge will probably have every right to reply—

"Because its' cow-hocked, lame on the off-hind and too big for your poor little kid who can't ride one side of it yet."

But being, like all judges, charming and tactful, he will undoubtedly answer—

"It's a charming pony—I've noticed him before—but he just wasn't going his best to-day. And your little girl—doesn't she ride well!—didn't seem able to make him show himself properly. Such a pity. I do hope you'll have better luck next time."

All with his fingers crossed. It won't do any good; she's out for blood. Her acknowledgement of his courtesy will echo across the show ground.

"Really! How extraordinary! Of course at the Seven Counties

G

Show General Bog-Spavin thought very highly of the pony indeed. But then *he* is a very experienced international judge, isn't he?"

And with this our judge will be left to contemplate Madame's tweeded rear half-acre as she storms majestically off, snorting fit to be hobdayed; though doubtless he would recommend that the incision should not be confined to the interior of her throat. Can you wonder that men have resigned the judging of ponies to the gentler sex?

Of course, not all Pony Club mothers are like that. The majority are anxious only that their child should enjoy the pony and are really interested in what the judge thinks of the combination. It is the latter-day Medusas who are concerned only incidentally with the pony and its wretchedly embarrassed rider; far more important is it for them that their ebulliently assumed superior status in the pony world should not be jeopardised by the insignificant and irrelevant opinion of some idiot whose sole qualification as a judge is a lifetime of hunting, racing, jumping, showing, breeding and loving horses. These harridans embrace also an indestructible conviction that the pony they own is—because they own it—outstanding in its class. Outstanding, that is, until they sell it. Then, it inevitably gets into bad hands and is immediately and irretrievably ruined; even though under the new management it proceeds to beat its replacement hands down in every show.

However, enough of the seamy side. Let us recall the fun, the colour and the thrills. The skill and showmanship of the driving classes from the dog-carts to the great road coaches with their finely matched teams of four. These are capped by the glamour and daring of the galloping musical drive of the guns of the King's Troop, Royal Horse Artillery and the intricate patterns of the Household Cavalry musical ride. The sight and sound of these glittering combinations thundering in exact manoevures round the arena are experiences to be recalled, compared and related to those who perhaps will not have the opportunity to be thrilled by them.

The pink coats of hunt staffs as they circle the ring with their hounds surging like the wash of a wave around them. The precise, strutting swagger of the hackneys; the flaring pride of the Arabians; the majesty and dignity of the big Shire horses and the Clydesdales and Percherons; the balance, acceleration and agility of the polo ponies; the austere pomp of the dressage arena; the ceremonious punctiliousness of the Hunt teams, immaculate in turn-out but not always so in performance; the music of the bands and the gay variety of the trade stands; all these contribute to the glamour, the atmosphere and the fascination of the horse show. And anyone whose pulse does not beat the faster in admiration and enjoyment of at least some part of such a programme is certainly no foxhunter, and must be indeed be so cold-blooded as to be virtually moribund.

When considering the relationship of the show hunters of the horse show to the hunters of the hunter trial we can consult with Colonel Williams again—

"In hunter shows, conformation and action are the most important factors; in hunter trials, performance, constitution and manners should be the main factors to decide the issue."

He goes on to say that unless conformation is taken into consideration in judging hunter trials—

"—the prizes may go to old, worn-out or misshapen horses that in spite of their performance are of little value. On the other hand, if too many marks are given for conformation, there is danger of the performance being overlooked and the prizes going to good-looking animals that are only indifferent performers."

Colonel Williams clearly identifies one of the main points of disagreement on the judging of hunter trials. Extremes of opinion exist on the subject. There are those who stress the importance of conformation and accept as inevitable by force of na-

❀

ture the implied consequence that a misshapen horse is "of little value" and even dangerous as a hunter. The strongest supporters of this wing are those who have a foot in both the camps of the hunter show and the hunter trials; to these the "value" of a hunter is not dependent on its ability across country, but more or less—according to the ambitions of its' owner —on its ability to show well and breed a similarly successful progeny.

At the other extreme are those who say that the horse which performs across country with the best manners and the greatest spirit and accuracy is patently the horse which one would prefer to hunt—never mind if it is old, misshapen or even blind in one eye. A hunting horse, according to this opinion, should be able to carry you through a hunt in any weather at any pace you wish to go, by the route you wish to take, with the greatest possible comfort to your person and to your peace of mind. If it isn't the most beautiful of the equine species, who cares? Let those with the horses supposedly of "more value" creep up long after the kill with their craven excuses of a little difficulty here and the need of a breather there. Who wants to lose his patience and risk his neck on some stupid, spiritless paragon of perfect symmetry?

The judges must naturally abide by the principles of scoring agreed by the committee which appoints them. Judges, after all, are usually competent and experienced in appreciating the qualities of a good hunter as interpreted by the committee in the entry schedule.and in the programme for the event; if they are not it is surely not they who are to blame, but the committee which selected them. It is worthwhile, in passing, to recommend that the qualities upon which entries will be judged are recorded in entry schedules and programmes. This is primarily for the benefit of the competitors, whose signature on the entry form certifies that they accept these along with the rest of the conditions of entry; though in my experience the majority sign without putting themselves to the trouble of reading anything other than the words "Sign here." This matters not in the least in most cases, since the vast majority of competitors accept the judges' decisions without question. But the committee and judges need a means of countering the hunter trial equivalents of the afore-described Medusa Mums; the type who inevitably regard any criticism of their ability as a malicious, personal affront and damn the judges as blind or stupid or both. These are the gentry who need their noses rubbed into the rules which they have by their entry accepted.

The method of judging at hunter trials depends almost entirely on the intervisibility of the obstacles and the number of the competitors. If all the obstacles can be seen from one stand and the entry is not too large, it is best to have the whole course judged from the one stand. At the other end of the scale is the situation where the chief judges can only see the first and last two fences, the remainder being lost from their view in a wood or behind a hill. In this event the local reserves of judging expertise will probably not run to the ratio of one expert per obstacle, and here the "knockable rail" is permissible, since an inexpert fence judge is then faced only with the uncomplicated problem of counting the number of times a competitor refuses at his fence and whether or not he knocked the rail down; his opinion on the horse's method of going about his business not being required. I suggest a "knockable rail" is an unnecessary form of obstacle on any other occasion, if for no other reason than that I have never met one in the hunting field—though I have met many breakable ones.

In some trials, speed, action and conformation have no bearing on the result, competitors being penalised only for knocking down "knockable rails" or refusals—and what constitutes a refusal can also be a matter for disagreement. This is one extreme of the scoring scale, favouring the careful slow coach who rarely extends into more than a ponderous canter. In other trials, faults incurred by knockdowns can be redeemed by completing the course by an equivalent number of seconds under a published standard time. This favours the bold, galloping horse which sometimes takes its chances over obstacles and is rarely the light-mouthed, patent-safety hunter for which the judges are supposed to be looking.

Within this wide bracket, there are many ingenious variations on the theme of a scoring scale, some of which are admittedly necessary to suit particular circumstances. I suggest the most reasonable solution is that the judges be asked to select the hunters they themselves would most prefer to ride across an average country—if, indeed, such a thing exists—remembering that the course designer has, or should have, supplied in the course the especial character of the local hunting country. And that the judges should then be presented with a scoring scale—if one is thought necessary—which will permit them to favour the horses which have the best action, which complete the course at a proper hunting pace for that particular country, which are well-mannered and biddable, and which have a pleasing conformation. The combination of these four elements based on the primary and overriding ability of the horse to complete a competent, safe round is surely the best means of producing the right result. However, this is by no means a rule, and, even if it were, there would always be admissible exceptions to it. Deciding on these is one of the chief responsibilities and interests of judging.

To close this sermon on judging I have two true stories.

On the first occasion, I was standing by a scoreboard at a hunter trials gloomily surveying the dismal details of how I had failed my excellent little horse, but inwardly congratulating the judges on their winning selections, when I heard an infuriated female voice behind me bray for everyone's—but particularly the assembled judges'—benefit.

"I think it's absolutely disgraceful that they marked poor

Mary down like that. She went clear in a very good time. She should have won it. That horse is a most difficult ride and she rode it quite beautifully."

Indeed the horse was patently a most difficult ride; and indeed, being a superlative horsewoman, Mary had ridden it beautifully. And as the judges very properly threw it out I expect they all said, as Mary did to me later that day—

"I'm glad I don't have to hunt that brute."

On the second occasion, I was standing with some strangers by one of the obstacles on a course. It was a three-foot upright, solid rail with an artificial dry ditch, five feet wide but only a foot deep, with a low guard rail toward you. A well built obstacle with the excellent quality, desirable in all hunter trial obstacles, of looking far more severe than it really was.

There appeared to be some delay as the next competitor was long in coming. Finally he appeared at a very slow canter; a large well-proportioned horse accompanied unevenly by a large, ill-proportioned rider. The horse trotted into both of the two fences before the one where I stood, clearing them both carefully and cleanly with a certain sedate grace. Breaking again into a slow canter he ponderously approached us. Fifteen yards out from the fence—with no assistance from his rider that I observed —he slowed into a trot, pounded over the guard rail and into the ditch, popped, almost from a standstill, neatly over the rail, walked several paces whilst his rider recovered from the ordeal, and then broke again into a stately canter. As he moved off the rider, wobbling horribly and clutching the neck strap of an entirely unnecessary breast-plate, turned and shouted in our direction—

"I'm clear so far, dear."

"Dear" turned to her companions.

"Isn't that good! He should win it, shouldn't he, if he goes clear?"

One of the companions made bold to reply—

"Well, the judges may not think he's going fast enough. It says in the programme that competitors must go at a fair hunting pace."

"Oh, fiddlesticks! That's what it always says," cries "dear," "What is a fair hunting pace? That's the pace he always goes hunting."

I was not competing myself, but sympathised somewhat with the many who were surprised and not a little annoyed when our inexpert cavalier was placed above other more competent riders whose horses had also gone clear, though not with such impeccable precision.

But what constitutes "a fair hunting pace?" We all have our own opinions, based principally on the type of country over which we are accustomed to hunt. If a judge is prepared to accept a deliberate, patent-safety progress as a fair hunting pace and you aren't—or can't manage one on your horse, though you would dearly like to—all you can do is to avoid the hunter trials at which such judges adjudicate.

However, we can't leave the matter there. Obviously, on both these occasions the rider affected the performance of the horse. In the first case a competent rider made an unsuitable hunter perform creditably—and was marked down; in the second a competent, good-looking horse performed creditably despite the hindrance of an incompetent rider, who, to give him credit, didn't lack courage,—and was marked up. If we remember again and agree with Colonel Williams' injunction that "performance, constitution and manners should be the main factors to decide the issue," we can have little argument with either of these decisions. Even if we don't agree with them. Though if you don't agree with them you might ask yourself which horse you would prefer to hunt.

After the judges, the course designers are the next most popular targets for criticism. The principles by which they work should be very simple; but sometimes are rather obscure.

I suggest that the first principle he, or she, should observe is to design a course to include a variety of the obstacles typical of the country hunted by the particular Hunt for whom the trials are organised. And if the most typical obstacle of that country is a "tiger-trap" or "chicken-coop" over wire, then the course should include a fair proportion of these, possibly varied in size, material and colour, but not so that they no longer resemble the genuine, native article; the wire on either side of the obstacle can be simulated by tarred string with knotted barbs if a little harmless realism is required.

Following on this, the second principle should be to lay out the course over as natural a piece of country as can be made available for the purpose. And the more natural obstacles—in addition to the typical—such as growing hedges, existing ditches, rails and stiles, which can be included in the course the better it will ride.

The third principle for course designers is to avoid steadfastly all desire to impress with a "clever" course. The aim should be to try to devise one easy enough for every competitor to get round, yet difficult enough to separate the sheep from the goats (this is not a very good simile—goats being usually cleverer and better jumpers than sheep) and provide the judges with not more than half-a-dozen to place finally by style of going, pace and manners.

Apart from the simple test of overcoming a series of obstacles in their path, the opening and shutting of gates and the slipping and replacement of slip-rails are a useful test of manners in a hunter; whilst the problems of awkward angles of approach, difficult take-offs and drops prove his cleverness and courage.

Lastly, course designers must resign themselves to the acceptance of the natural fact that they cannot please everyone; remembering that competitors and spectators judge obstacles from the viewpoint of their own horse—or rather, what they think it is, the viewpoint of a horse often changing remarkably with a change of rider.

For the course builder, who is not always the course designer, there are three principles which he can with advantage observe. Firstly, he will save himself labour and temper on the day if he builds as solidly as his time and material will allow. Secondly, he should, for his own convenience, so construct each timber obstacle that it can be easily and quickly dismantled; this has the added advantage of permitting the easier extraction of the unfortunate who up-ends inextricably in the middle of the double oxer. And thirdly, he should be prepared for every obstacle which can be shattered—which means every obstacle—to be shattered, repeatedly, and to provide plenty of spare material at each site to meet recurrent emergencies.

He should also be prepared for the judges to demand that the first three fences be completely rebuilt five minutes before the first competitor is due to start; and when so confronted should curb his desire to invite the judges to do this themselves.

Let him also remember, when he has dismantled his course, to store his timber securely. Otherwise, when next year, short of time as usual, he seeks it for the new course, he may discover to his confusion, discomfort and expense that it has been purloined for fence posts, milk churn ramps, silage pitwalls, hunt jumps or just plain fire wood. However he should not store it so securely as to forget where he put it; this too can be confusing, discomforting and expensive.

There remain the committee, who fondly believe that they have had to cope with all the preparation and administration, and the secretary who knows that he, or she, has. By the day of the trials he can usually be heard swearing that this is the very last time he is going to do it too, and next year "they" can get someone else to run their damned errands for them, etc. etc. Next year, having succumbed to heavy and repeated applications of soft soap, he is either at it again, or, if he is clever, has become one of "them."

The prime essential quality required in a secretary of a hunter trial, or any other equine event, is the ability to remember always to count to ten before answering. This will preserve his sanity and earn him an envied reputation for imperturbability. Everything else about his job he can only learn from experience —generally fun, sometimes infuriating and frustrating, but always fascinating.

The only attributes required of a committee, having delivered itself of its considered directions for the conduct of the trials, are blind faith in and unquestioning support for the secretary. They also need to know when to get out of the way and stay there; just within earshot of the secretary's shout for help.

Competitors, in my experience, vary from the immensely competent to the utterly cretinous. One can frequently tell who is going to be which from the way they fill in their entry forms. One can also sometimes judge how well a competitor will perform over the course by observing how he performs in the collecting ring. Waiting in the collecting ring for one's turn to go tends to hone an edge on the nerves. It is noticeable that the relaxed and experienced competitor is commonly the one to remember that the disconsolate figure, standing stolidly at the entrance to the ring in the pouring rain, endlessly checking numbers on a slowly disintegrating mill-board, is not doing it for his own particular honour and glory, nor even to satisfy his own peculiar form of masochism, and treats him and all his fellow helpers with the courtesy their unselfishness deserves.

But at hunter trials, far more than at horse shows, it is the spectators who set the stage, who generate the atmosphere, who make the day. The judge on his wagon, binoculars glued under the rim of his bowler hat, is remote as Caesar on his chariot scanning all three parts of Gaul. The competitors, oblivious to encouragement and catcall, stride more or less determinedly on their way; like all competitors, they are, for the moment, alone on earth. The secretary and his assistants are buzzing like any hive, organising and reorganising, ordering and counter-ordering, counting and miscounting, introspective and insensible to all time and events unconnected with the trials. And above it all the steady burble of the commentator, inevitably interrupted from time to time by electronic belch or whistle, drones on like some mystic incantation, incomprehensible to anyone more than five yards from the few loudspeakers which are working.

Through the day the spectators wander, rubber booted or sensibly shod, laden with binoculars, shooting sticks and cameras, round the course; some one way, some the other, some entirely and happily aimlessly. They cluster in eager anticipation round the fences most likely to cause confusion and disaster; cheering and groaning, craning and peering, gossiping and wondering—" when old George is coming round on that horrible monster of his."

Finally, wearied with the exertions and emotions of the day, they sprawl on rugs or on the tailgates of station wagons amid the litter of wicker baskets, thermos containers, bottles, cardboard plates, silver foil and greaseproof paper. Here then with omniscient expertise they decide the fates of nations or consign them to the rubbish bag along with the picked chicken legs. Here the locally elected representative of government is eviscerated, so to speak, with a plastic picnic knife; the intricacies of county politics determined with the flourish of a ham sandwich; the secretary, committee and all concerned with the conduct of the hunter trials torn metaphorically limb from limb and all their many transgressions laid bare. Here there is much talk of—

"Well, of course, if I was running things . . ." from the many who never intend to expose themselves to that danger.

At the end of the day, "as the sun sinks slowly in the west"— because somehow, even if it has rained all day at a hunter trial the weather always seems to clear in the evening—everyone sits around relaxing gratefully and waiting. Waiting for the final results; for the outcome of the squabble about whether old Thingummy went the wrong side of the finishing flag; for someone to give us a hand getting this blasted horse into the trailer; for the tractor to tow us out of this bloody bog. Or just waiting until the bottle is empty. It's been a great day.

"Now next year I think we ought to . . ."

Still Earlier Mornings

IF IN MID SUMMER you think you, or, with the approach of cub-hunting, your horse, could do with a little exertion to help dissipate what Mr. Delme Radcliffe MFH calls "inside fat," I can think of no better advice than to suggest that you ask permission to accompany hounds on exercise.

You can exercise hounds on foot, on a horse or on a bicycle; that is, of course, you are on the bicycle or horse—hounds have difficulty reaching the pedals.

The form is first to ask the Master. He will say—

"Yes, of course. Delighted if you would help. I can't get out as often as I would like. Will you see Tom about it?" and leave the rest to you.

The next step is to go to the kennels. Tom, the kennel-huntsman, will say—

"Very happy to have you come along, sir. We'll be walking

'em out tomorrow morning if you care to come to kennels at five, sir?"

"Walking out? On foot? At five?" You try to say all this nonchalantly, as though you expected it.

"That's right, sir," says Tom, a little maliciously, knowing full well you hadn't. "We like to get 'em out early, before it gets hot and while there's not much traffic about."

You wonder whether a few press-ups and a knee bends or two in the morning wouldn't do just as well. You don't have to get out of bed at four in the morning to do those. But it's too late. You're committed.

There you are at five in the morning, standing by the grass yard gate, in a gentle, warm drizzle, wondering how you are going to stay awake at the rather pompous dinner party in the evening. Confidentially, that is the least of your worries. Just remember to say to your hostess as soon as possible after your arrival and loudly enough for everyone else to hear—

"Sorry if I seem dull to-night, I was out exercising hounds at five this morning." That will explain everything, including falling asleep in your soup; but remember to say it before you do; it doesn't sound nearly so effective through a table napkin soggy with Brown Windsor. If your hostess replies gaily to your opening gambit—

"Oh really? I hadn't noticed any difference." Don't take umbrage. She probably means it politely. If, however, one of the guests says it—well, it is always helpful to know who your enemies are.

Back to the grass yard gate. There you stand watching the hounds circling, playing, rolling, galloping hither and yon and rearing up against the wire fence shouting at you to hurry and let them out. Your cap is down over your eyes, your hands are deep in your pockets and your shoulders hunched against the weather. You think of the warm bed you have left. The drizzle oozes over your fourth vertebra.

Tom comes bustling round the corner of the fence. Ben, the second whip, strides down the yard. Their cheery alertness shames you out of your misery and you try to look more alive than you feel.

"If you'll just stand over there, sir," says Tom, "They'll come out a bit sharp like, so you don't want to be in their way. Right, Ben. Let 'em on."

Ben pushes his way through the hounds.

"Get back Marvel! Get back Somerset, get back will you! How the hell d'you think I'm going to open the gate with your fat backside in the way. Get back! You too, Thrasher. Get on out of it."

He heaves the gate open against the weight of the close packed hounds and out they pour, squeezing, shoving, leaping over one another in a tumble of tan, white and black. Most rush over to where Tom stands, calling them quietly by name as they surge round him. Some swing over to have a look at you, more out of curiosity than courtesy.

"Hold up, all of you. Hold up then," says Tom conversationally. "Hold up, Paragon, where d'you think you're off to? Get down Merriment! Linkboy—hold up, will you!"

Ben slams and secures the yard gate behind him. He walks quickly on beyond Tom and turns about to face us, walking slowly backwards. He whistles and calls the hounds on—

"Paragon! Pageant! Cope, lads."

The hounds named move towards him followed by the rest of the pack. As they come up to him he turns and strides off, the lash of his whip flicking across in front of the noses of the leading hounds to hold them in check behind him.

"Now, sir," says Tom, "if you'll come along of me I'll name hounds to you as we go. There's some as you don't know and quite a few you may have forgotten, I shouldn't wonder."

Though my memory is the despair of my associates, I have never had any difficulty in learning and remembering the names

Circling, rolling, galloping hither and yon

of hounds. The first and easiest feature for recognition is, of course, the colour. But many hounds share the same pattern of colour, so this means can often be misleading particularly at a distance. The trick, I was taught, is to study the way the hound moves and carries itself; and to learn how it speaks. It fascinates me how when, with a minor gale blowing and the width of a thick wood between them, a huntsman will listen to a solitary hound speak faintly once and say—

"That damn Sextant! What he's babbling on about I'm sure I don't know. And he don't neither, I warrant you!"

or, on the other hand—

"Hark to old Counsellor there!" A pause, and the hound speaks again more insistently. "Counsellor's got it. Hark to Counsellor! Hark to Counsellor all of you!"

—and be right both times.

And then again, when turning the corner of a covert with one of the whippers-in, you see one hind leg and the stern of a hound disappear round the next corner three hundred yards away. The whipper-in will swear,

"There's bloody Tarquin skirting again. We ought to knock him on the head, straight we ought." And when we get up with the hound it is indeed Tarquin and he slinks into the covert away from the whip's rate.

It comes from a real love for hounds and understanding of how they think. This is not learned from the study of pedigrees and books on hound management, but by being with and observing hounds in kennel and out at exercise. One never learns exactly how any hound will behave in the hunting field this way; but one will get a very good idea. For those who ride to hunt there is no better way of increasing your enjoyment of a day's hunting than by this sort of knowledge of the hounds you follow. And such an acquaintance enables you, in times of crisis and a divided pack, to offer valuable help to the hunt staff.

However, there you are, striding alongside Tom behind the

hounds, feeling a touch better now that you are on the move, and your instruction begins.

"Now this bitch here by me is Silence, entered last season and done well, she did. Bit light you'd say and her neck's on the short side too. Statesman there, you can always tell him by the white line between his shoulders, he's out of the same litter; and so's Stamper, him with the black saddle, he's a good sort. Takes after his sire old Pageant up in front there. Always in front those two Pageant and Paragon. Good hunting hounds those two, sir, go all day they will; they're the devil to stop when you want to. They're by Blankly Chaplain out of our Parasol, that old dark bitch what's getting under your feet there; get on Parasol girl!—can't abide roads, she can't, sir, her feet's none too good, poor old girl, but get her on grass and she ruddy flies." And so on. At the end of the exercise your head is full, so to speak, of Parasol's feet, Stamper's saddle and Silence's short neck and you wonder if you will ever get them straight. You find yourself looking forward to the next time you are invited to be at the kennels at five in the morning and wondering why it was all so difficult earlier.

Other enjoyable mornings follow and you feel much the better for them. By now you have got some names and their associated colour, shape and characteristics straight. It's a great day when for the first time you pluck up your courage enough to say—

"Hold up, Daystar."

Of course, it better had be Daystar. Nothing so shatters the morale of the tyro amateur whipper-in than the contemptuous gaze of a hound so addressed that is not Daystar. The message comes over clearly—

"Who the hell's the idiot calling Daystar. Daystar's not even out this morning."

And the rest of the pack all grin or drop their heads and snigger. But if the hound looks up in recognition and moves to obey, your day is made.

Then comes the day when Tom says—

"We'll be needing to give 'em a bit faster work on the road from now on, sir. Have you got a bicycle? If you haven't you can always borrow my missus's."

As it happens you haven't, and you feel a bit of a clown trundling about on Mrs. Tom's ancient ladies' model; especially when you find it hasn't any brakes. However, you pedal sturdily along thinking about how much good this is doing your riding muscles and listening, as usual, to Tom on the subject of the qualities or misdeeds of his hounds, spiced with an occasional horrific piece of gossip gleaned from the hunt staff grape vine.

The road narrows and a tipper truck lumbers towards the pack from the opposite direction. You pedal sharply towards Stentor and Stoker, who are engaged in examining a drain on the wrong side of the road. You swing your whip throng free and forward to crack it. The world wheels suddenly around you and you land on the road on your back with the bicycle on top of you.

The pack, as one hound, rushes to help, and you are revived with a slobber of tongues. In the dim distance you hear Tom rating hounds fiercely and you think hazily to yourself that this is the first time you have ever heard him really angry with them. The bicycle is lifted off you and you are raised bodily by Tom, Ben and the lorry driver.

"You all right, sir? Sit down on the bank a minute. Cor, you took a right old toss there."

Then more cheerfully—

"Can't see no blood anywhere. Must have shook you up a bit though. Would you like Harry here to run you home, sir—he's going by your way?"

Harry is the driver of the lorry and a keen follower of the hunt, like most of the folk round here.

"No, thank you, all the same" you say, "I'm feeling quite OK." You get up a bit stiffly and untangle the thong of your whip jammed solidly around three spokes and the front fork of the bicycle. You have learned your lesson and next time you halt your bicycle before letting fly your lash.

Shortly after this disaster comes the most enjoyable sort of hound exercise; the sort you had had in mind when first you asked to accompany the hounds. It means getting up an hour earlier because now you have to hack the four miles to the kennels on the mare.

The drill is still the same. Ben is out in front with the thong of his whip occasionally waving in front of the over-eager noses of the usual leaders—Paragon and Pageant and three or four others. They are always up there trying to push past Ben, now on one side, now on the other, and you can hear him talking quietly to them as he jogs on, tuning to his right in his saddle to look down on them—

"Paragon, hold up, will you. You too, Pageant," the red lash of his whip snaps exactly in front of Pageant's nose and the hound checks in his stride. Ben catches another hound creeping up on his left.

"Rampart," and again, a little more threateningly, "Rampart!" Rampart drops his head and ducks behind Ben's horse. Back again to the right to find a new hound neck and neck with Pageant.

"Temptress, what are you doing up here, girl. You're learning bad habits from that old devil."

The red lash flicks out and this time catches Pageant on the flank behind the elbow. Pageant stops in his tracks with a yelp and barges his way to safety behind Ben's horse's heels. Temptress takes the hint and drops back into the middle of the pack.

As you trot along at a quiet hound jog behind them, the characters of individual hounds are revealed more clearly than before. There are the inveterate leaders, always on Ben's heels or flanks. There are the skirters, like the causes of your downfall on the bicycle, Stentor and Stoker, always out to a side, always curious to know what lies under that hedge or in that drain, always searching for interesting scent; these will often be the keenest hounds in the hunting field and the surest noses in the pack.

There are "the good guys," padding along quietly in the main body, honest, cheerful and hardworking, rarely in trouble. And then there is always the "riot squad," so named not because it disciplines or disperses the rioters within the pack, but because, given half a chance, its members will, either singly or in a ravening rabble, riot after anything from a cat to a cow, fight, mob up and generally misbehave more quickly than you can ever get your whip thong swinging. A very few will act with malice aforethought and vicious intent; such, no matter how well they work in the hunting field, you can do without. But the majority of the riot squad are high spirited buffoons who accept a rating and a cut round the rear with your lash as all part of the game. Such a one is old Patriot padding stolidly along on your side of the main body of the "good guys"; now and again turning his head to leer up at you, gauging the level of your attention. The sight of the chimneys of "The Plough Inn" ahead gives you the clue to his thoughts—

"You think you've got us all buttoned up in a nice tidy little bunch, don't you, matey? Well, if that fat old tomcat is asleep on the steps of 'The Plough" again—are you going to get shook up!"

Sure enough as you approach "The Plough" the centre of gravity of the riot squad shifts your way. A few heads come up —among them Patriot's—and a few shifty glances switch quickly between your direction and "The Plough." If you can see the damned cat you will be wise to push up a little alongside the pack and warn Patriot to have a care, possibly supporting this with a slow circling swing of your whip, on your off-side. Patriot's sly smirk is replaced by an expression of wide-eyed innocence and the riot squad disperses.

On you jog, along field paths and through little used lanes. The post office van pulls into the side under the hedge and the driver calls cheerily to Tom. The big blue milk float, collecting the churns from the farm gates backs into a yard to clear your way and the driver, his mate and a farmhand greet you as you pass. At the main road crossing in the village the policeman, cycling slowly along to the local station, stops and halts the little traffic until you are all across. The post office driver, the driver of the milk float and his mate, the farmhand and the policeman are all local country-folk. Whether they actively support the Hunt or not—and most do—they have always shared with their forbears a very special feeling for the hounds, whose activities throughout the year play an essential part in the countryman's calendar.

Over the main road, along the rutted chalk track which climbs the side of the down, and on to the crest of the downland turf, where the tattered shadow patches of the flying clouds chase each other across the gorse and the wind thrums in our ears and tangles the manes and tails of the horses. Down into the shelter of the valley to the big paddock adjoining the kennels where Tom calls a halt. He drops his reins, cocks his legs forward of his saddle flaps, lights a cigarette and sits, elbows on knees, cigarette shielded in the cup of his hand, watching his hounds sunning themselves, playing and rolling. He calls single hounds to him, throwing them bits of biscuit and talking to them gently. Our horses take their chance too and, heads down, pull at the lush meadow grass.

Finally, nipping out the stub between finger and thumb, blackened and hardened with this practice, Tom rides slowly over to the entrance to the grass yard. Here he dismounts, hands his reins to Ben and opening the hatch of the salt splash, checks hounds through and into the enclosure. The "riot squad" bored at thought of the long day in kennels, crowd to the fence grinning at him and shouting ruderies. He pushes his fingers through the wire netting and gently pinches their noses whilst they mouth his hand.

"Never you mind, my beauties," he says, "Never you mind. We'll all be out cubbing in a month's time."

The Image of War

" 'Unting . . . is the sport of Kings—the image of war without it's guilt, and only five and twenty per cent of it's danger"
—*J. Jorrocks M.F.H.*

This analogy of Mr. Jorrocks' is enthusiastically supported by the soldier, who in peace—and even in war—traditionally has had recourse to foxhunting to occupy his leisure hours. Originally, perhaps, this was regarded as a proper compliance with the instruction of Queen's Regulations (Queen Victoria's that is) that young officers should be encouraged to live dangerously. The object being thereby to sharpen their reactions in dangerous situations and so improve their ability to lead in battle; though, on occasion, it did lead to the premature demise of some unfortunates.

In these soberer and less spirited times this instruction appears to have been amended to encouragement to live industriously and strive for qualifications. The object now being, presumably, to ensure an ability to write a military paper, appropriately punctuated and replete with the correct abbreviations. The casualties resulting from this change of stress are attributable not so much to initiative and daring as to boredom and ulcers.

A study of Baily's Hunting Directory reveals the interesting facts that the majority of packs of hounds raised abroad were founded by soldiers; and also that soldiers—regular or territorial—form a considerable proportion of the Masters of Hounds, past and present, in this country and elsewhere. At the head of their distinguished ranks stands, naturally, the Iron Duke himself; though I can't find any reference in Baily's to the pack of hounds he maintained during the Peninsular War within the safety of the defensive lines of Torres Vedras. Perhaps they were called the TVH—or just the Torres Vedras. And one can imagine the description which would have accompanied this title had it ever appeared in Baily's; unquestionably drafted by the Commander-in-Chief himself—

"A rolling country, somewhat steep and rocky in parts, with small coverts affording excellent views and fields of fire. It encompasses some hundred square miles enclosed on the west and south by the Atlantic Ocean, on the east by the River Tagus and on the north by the rear echelons of the 1st and 4th Divisions. A well-bred, short-legged horse is the best sort, preferably accustomed to cannon-fire and handy enough to avoid the fall of spent shot. Covert hacks are not desirable, since, in the event of emergency, all available horse-holders will be immediately required for other duties. Gentlemen may attend in any suitable form of dress but must invariably be equipped as for skirmishing order. At every Meet gentlemen will please to present their arms and accoutrements for inspection by the Field Master before hounds move off. No subscriptions and no caps are required. Times and venues of Meets will be published in General Orders. Best centres:—Lisbon and Mafra."

Earlier than this, across the Atlantic, a no less distinguished soldier and excellent horseman, General George Washington, had his own pack of hounds which he hunted in Virginia, and to which the French Revolutionary General and patriot the Marquis de Lafayette, himself a keen hunting man, had contributed three and a half couple of French hounds as his personal gift. And, still in America, at a later date, that embodiment of the United States Cavalry, General George Patton, was renowned as a good man to hounds with a characteristically colourful turn of phrase when expressing his displeasure to the field. At the other end of the scale, so to speak, it may come as a surprise to some critics of the German military character to learn that the cavalry and artillery of the German Central Group of Armies invading Russia in 1941 had with them no less than six packs of hounds.

So one cannot claim that a dedication to hunting was ever confined to the British Army; though, not surprisingly, where ever our Army has sat for long, bored with inactivity and dreaming of home, packs of hounds have materialised. Their titles sound romantically strange; as was the way, one supposes, some of them hunted. The Peshawar Vale, the Ootacamund, the Bombay Bobbery, the Poona, the Royal Exodus. I find them intriguing enough, but, to diverge for a moment from our military theme on to the subject of names, for sheer colour and delight—or amazement—try some Americana,—the Battle Creek, the Chagrin Valley, the Iroquois, the Foxcatcher—and, not least, the Casanova.

My own experience of hunting with British military packs abroad has been confined to Italy and Germany.

In Italy we hunted the country around Trieste and Sesana. This was in 1946, when the ownership of the area was in dispute, and with the war fresh in our memory, there was little regard for life and limb. The main hazards, other than those naturally inherent in the sport, were the ever present opportunities of either disappearing for ever down one of the supposedly volcanic and apparently bottomless funnels in the rocks, used by the local inhabitants for the disposal of garbage and unwanted relatives, which yawned in front of one with alarming ubiquity and frequency; or of being selected by the Jugoslav border patrols as a mark for their moving target practice.

Since it's arrival in Western Germany in 1945, the half of the British Army which has existed there from that date has constantly endeavoured to maintain, with varying degrees of success, a variety of packs of hounds. In certainty of contradiction I would suggest that the Warman, the Rezegh and the Wessex Hounds, all now regrettably disbanded, were probably the most renowned of these; and not for the quality of hunting alone, their effect on the canine population of North Germany, in both numbers and variety can still be remarked.

Unfortunately, apart from the inevitable restrictions imposed by the expense of this pastime, and the amount, or rather lack, of spare time available to the hunt staffs—all serving soldiers—a further restriction exists in the shape of the German law forbidding the organised pursuit of one animal by another. It is widely alleged that this law was the concept of Herman Goering—no sort of horseman—who, clad incongruously in a hunting costume of his own design, usually defined as Robin Hood in tights with a shaving brush in his hat, was as one might expect, a regular devotee of that organized massacre, the battue. In consequence of this devotion the law still permits the hunting of game by dogs only for the benefit of the shooter.

However, despite these restrictions, Germany remains for me the most rewarding of the military environments in which I have hunted.

When, on arriving in Wessex Barracks in Fallingbostel in 1964, the Royal Scots Greys decided to reform the Wessex Hounds—founded and kennelled there originally by the Queen's Bays in 1946—we met with the kindest and most generous encouragement from everyone we approached. The Cottesmore, the Pytchley, the Middleton, the Buccleuch and the Linlithgow and Stirlingshire all gave us drafts, a surprisingly even lot considering the number of kennels from which they came; the Eglinton gave us our couple of comedians, Actor and Daystar. Then, immediately the British and German ministerial authorities—export, import, veterinary, customs—the gamut— began to place their ingeniously frustrating obstacles in our path and the inevitable paperwork piled high. But to the determined soldier authoritarian obstacles present no problem. He learns to overcome them by a judicious use of deceit or feigned ignorance or both. Nevertheless to avoid embarrassments—and possible legal harassments—it is better that the saga of the voyage of the Wessex Hounds from their English and Scottish kennels to Fallingbostel remains a military secret.

But however undaunted by authority the determined soldier-huntsman may be, it is the conquest of the problems presented by Nature which really tax him, demanding other skills than those acquired at Staff College. One may study the theory of the solution of natural problems by reading books. One only learns the technique by practical experience—with the Furies in close attendance.

Take for instance the near disaster which threatened the Wessex Hounds on their first day's hunting after their re-formation by the Greys. They were to hunt a drag, which, on the day before the opening meet we had planned, with the Forst-meister's assistance, to run over a nice line of fences across open fields, and so avoid the deer and wild pig skulking in the local woods. The interests of the Forstmeister—who approximates to a State-employed, glorified head gamekeeper—were served by this plan. He would be responsible, at a later date, for ensuring that these same deer and pig appeared in adequate numbers and in the right places before the guns of various important Ministerial guests. His interests were further served by the gift of a bottle of brandy.

The following day we got hounds to the Meet accompanied by an international and expectant throng, expectant of what they were not quite sure, and nor were we. After a wait of fifteen minutes, whilst the runner with the drag got away, we put hounds on. In theory I was hunting hounds that day and in practice—for the first mile—I did. After that Diana took over, and Diana is not the name of my wife.

At the end of that first mile, on peering between the ears of my horse whilst recovering from a disagreement on where to take off over a hideous chasm, I observed with misgiving that hounds appeared to be swinging from the prepared line towards the southern side of a wood. In my ignorance I had not realized how much that morning's change in the direction and strength of the wind would affect the lie of a scent laid as little as ten minutes before. I now appreciated that the scent had been carried, at least in part, to the southern and sunny edge of the wood, where the deer would be contentedly couched—but not for long.

My appreciation—unlike most of my military appreciations— proved entirely accurate, and was quickly confirmed by a remarkable change in the note and pace of the hounds. Until then they had been happily bumbling along the familiar aniseed line—and if anyone ever tells you that hounds won't hunt anything else after they have been introduced to aniseed, never believe them—now they let fly as if every fox brush in Christendom was tickling their noses.

The wood was an unthinned plantation of young fir, too thick to penetrate with ease on foot, let alone on a horse. There was nothing we could do but ring it and try to stop hounds as they came out. The deer came out like confetti, but enough stayed in the wood to keep hounds amused. And hounds, obviously appreciating their advantage over us, raced up and down and through the wood, deaf to whip, rate and horn. They made a glorious noise, which would have been more enjoyable if we had intended it.

The Forstmeister, fuming, approached me at the double. He was under the impression that I had purposely put hounds into the wood. He said he would immediately return to his house, get his gun, and shoot all hounds chasing deer if I did not at once remove them. A very clear and forceful statement, I thought. However it presented only an authoritarian obstacle and one applied the standard formula.

"Herr Forstmeister!" I cried in evident anxiety and in-different German, "You are very experienced in hunting. Please help us protect your deer." A moment's total incomprehension, then—you could almost hear the thought process going on in his head—"This British cavalry officer is asking me for help!"—his manner changed on the instant.

"Jawohl, Herr Oberst!" he cried, and turning, launched himself across the ditch and into the wood like a tank. Moments later, scratched, sweating but beaming, he emerged dragging a very surprised but abjectly subdued Daystar.

"Ein Hund!" he shouted triumphantly, "Vun off your togs. Goot tog!"

Daystar looked at him with amazed disbelief. The Forst-meister smiled happily.

"I like the Hunt, Herr Oberst. Is very interestink."

He plunged back into the wood again like a spaniel into a swamp. If he'd had a tail he'd have been wagging it.

I had supposed that this unplanned harassment of the deer would also antagonize the local farmers, but was relieved to find it had the exactly opposite effect. The farmer on whose land we were, greeted me with a broad smile as I circled the wood.

"Your hounds hunt very well, Herr Oberst. They will chase away the deer and pig that do so much damage to my fields."

As on the last occasion we had visited his farm, ostensibly on exercise, they had chased his sister and her pet cat on to the roof of his pig pen, I welcomed this apparent improvement in their public image. And though I knew that the farmers resented not being permitted to shoot over their land, all game being the property of the State, this—for us—advantageous aspect of rioting on to deer hadn't struck me before. Thereafter we used this argument regularly, and usually successfully, in excusing the sadly recurrent mis-behaviour of our "togs".

My morale was finally restored to me by the courtesy of the Divisional Commander, whom I found busily assisting in stopping hounds on the far side of the wood. In reply to my apology for the debacle he replied cheerfully,

"Good heavens, my dear chap, I'm enjoying myself enormously. It's just like hunting in Surrey."

It was kind of him but I couldn't think what he meant, because I've never had the pleasure of hunting in Surrey.

On a later occasion Nature presented us with a problem to which I doubt she has subjected any other Master of Hounds. Returning to kennels after an unusual afternoon's hunting—that is, one which went according to plan—I was smugly congratulating myself that perhaps we were at last getting things right. The whip having had to go home early to do something military, I was leading hounds and the kennelman was bicycling along behind them.

As we jogged through a small village the local policeman ponderously pedalled his bicycle towards us. We exchanged salutes and sonorous "Guten abends". As he passed I could not fail to detect a strong meaty scent of hot garlic sausage. This did not surprise me.

Trotting on, musing on the day's success, I was brought

sharply to earth by the all-too-familiar scurrying noise behind me and the kennelman's frantic shout—followed immediately by the policeman's angry bellow. Hounds had rioted on to a large packet on the carrier of the policeman's bicycle, which they were now dismembering with all the guttural scrimmaging and striving usually reserved for the breaking up of a fox.

We got our whips going at once. I couldn't think what to shout.—" 'Ware sausage!" seemed appropriate but hardly dignified enough. But it was all too late. The parcel had disappeared, string, paper and all.

I looked over to the policeman, expecting to see him, pistol out, demanding to execute all the hounds on the spot. This would not have surprised me either. I was amazed to see him doubled up on a nearby window-sill, slapping his fat thighs and shaking with laughter. Recovering himself slightly, he gasped between wheezes,

"Ach, Herr Oberst, your hounds hunt like demons. Gott verdammt! They chase the pig in a sausage as well as alive!"

Overcome by the brilliance of his wit he collapsed again, this time into a paroxysm of volcanic hiccups.

In dour silence the Scots kennelman picked up the policeman's bicycle. When the policeman could finally stand unassisted by the wall, we led him, giggling weakly, back to the meatshop-cum-beerhouse where we bought a replacement sausage and a beer all round. Hounds, strangely, took no interest in the meat-shop. I suspect they were beginning to regret the garlic sausage. The kennelman reported later that the hounds that hadn't been out that day wouldn't speak to them for over a week. And thereafter the policeman became hysterical whenever he met us.

I suppose things do go just a little wrong in the best of the well-established packs. But whenever some Master has kindly invited me to visit his kennels and accompany hounds on exercise, I have always been impressed to the point of reverence at their state of well-ordered calm and discipline.

Well-ordered calm and discipline are, of course, supposed to be the hall-marks of all efficient military establishments. But I can't remember them ever being distinctive features of any military pack of my acquaintance. I wonder what problems the Iron Duke had with his?

Try back

"DON'T EXPECT them to hunt the way we do," said my prede-
cessor, "Things are very different over here."

I had just arrived in Washington for a two year appointment
with the Army Staff of our Embassy and was ready to accept
unquestioningly any guidance on the American way of life.
After one hunting season I appreciate what he meant. Now,
when my English friends ask me what the hunting is like in the
United States, my answer is—"It's great fun but it's different,"
—and that is not just the part-time diplomat in me.

How is it different? Let me explain. But first let me say that
my hunting has been confined to the states of Maryland and
Virginia, and, though this is the heartland of fox hunting in
America, the conditions and circumstances and practices of the
twenty eight hunting countries contained by these states are by

no means identical with those of the other seventy five, as listed in Baily's Hunting Directory, elsewhere in the United States.

Fox hunting in the United States is largely confined to the eastern states; Virginia, Pennsylvania, Maryland and New York states having the most packs; though Hunts exist in twenty six of the forty eight continental states, including some in the far west. The fox hunting area of the eastern states alone is roughly fifteen hundred miles by one thousand miles and covers the variations in temperature and weather between the latitudes of 30° N to 45° N, that is, on the eastern side of the Atlantic, from Cairo to the Alps; the temperature during the last hunting season in Virginia alone having varied from 85° to 24° Fahrenheit. And since I have, so to speak, only hunted the area around Greece, it would be wrong for me to do more than generalise.

Now the differences. Firstly, what we in England call "hunting" is in America called "fox-hunting"; "hunting" being what we would call "shooting." You may think this irrelevant. You're wrong. In the hunting season any American hunter, properly licensed, is permitted by law an infinitely greater freedom of destruction than any similarly unpropertied or unsyndicated sportsman in England. This generous and traditional dispensation by the government, apart from permitting a certain degree of dangerous inexpertise, does nothing to increase the sadly depleted red fox population.

In dealing with the more practical differences a few original quotations may add a little local flavour to my assessment.

"They hunt the best goddam jungle outside of the Congo." (*Virginian cocktail party chatter*)

The one and a half million square miles comprising the hunting countries of the eastern United States provides, you will appreciate, in addition to variations of temperature and weather, some variety of terrain. Within the countries it can range from immaculately farmed areas—largely in the north—to the secondary jungle of the old plantations—largely in the south; from flat, river valley pasture and an occasional few acres of plough to steep, close-ranged hills resembling parts of the English West or Border countries.

Most coverts are woodland, a five-hundred acre wood being regarded as very small here. In the southern woodlands the foliage, even in winter is far heavier than anything seen in England. Only in the more extensively farmed states of the north are smaller coverts found, and the kale and other winter greens which commonly provide fox-lodging in England cannot survive the winter except in the most southern of the United States.

In the woodlands, deer—and a variety of other game, including bear—abound, and breaking hounds of such interesting riot is neither easy nor permanent in effect, especially in the thicker woods and steep hills of the south where close control of hounds is difficult.

So my second difference is, that here it is usually harder for hounds to find a fox and, having found, to hold to him and push him out into the open. However, once out in the open the countries are almost entirely permanent grassland and a joy to ride. The fences are usually rails or "chicken coops" (less, thank Heaven, the chickens) and are straight-forward and inviting, though sometimes alarming in size and substance. Hedges, cut-and-laid, stake-and-bound or just natural are, unfortunately, few. But so, fortunately, are "awkward places." This term, for the benefit of American readers, is the British hunting correspondents' customary description of some yawning, seemingly bottomless, black chasm, surmounted from an impossibly unsound take-off on to an inaccessible and precarious landing. Hunting correspondents frequently observe proceedings from a car or on foot, and so have the leisure to watch others enjoying these typically British obstacles.

"There's nothing so queer as scent, 'cept a woman." (*John Jorrocks Esq. MFH—not an original American source*)

According to the records the average monthly rainfall in the eastern United States is approximately the same as in England. Personally I find this hard to believe. However, the longer, hotter summers and autumns dry out the ground more than is the case in England. Masters with experience of hunting hounds on both sides of the Atlantic complain that scenting conditions in America are usually not so good as in the British Isles, and blame the comparative dryness of the soil. On the other hand, since for the most part the land is not so intensively cultivated as in England, and there are fewer roads, there is probably less artificial foil.

I hazard no opinion other than Mr Jorrocks', since I am well aware that the second quality shared by scent and a woman is that no two men can ever agree entirely about either.

Our third difference then is that, scent being frequently poor, hounds need more help from the huntsman than would be usual in England; though there are, admittedly, a few parts of the British Isles, and indeed a few parts of most of the hunting countries therein, where scent is always bad. In America the difficult coverts too frequently forbid the huntsman ever getting close enough to help his hounds, so the hounds must have the determination and drive to hold to a catchy scent and work it out for themselves. Which brings me on to the disputatious subject of hounds.

"I aim to breed the sort of hound that can hunt the country I have to hunt the way I want it hunted." (*A Virginian MFH*)

There are three main types of fox hound in America. The imported English hound, the Anglo-American cross-bred and the American hound—of which there are several, distinctive minor strains.

Opinions vary—occasionally rather heatedly—on the value of their qualities. Disputation is however, to use an American expression, counter-productive. Countries vary and the aim of any MFH must surely be that so clearly and concisely expressed in the quotation with which I head this paragraph. The decision on which hounds to use is best left to the man who knows what he needs to do the work. For those interested in pursuing this subject further I would suggest study of the well-argued and informative letter of Mr W. W. Brainard Jr, Joint Master of the Old Dominion Hounds, which appeared in "Horse and Hound" in May 1967.

Perhaps the Green Spring Valley Hunt entry in Baily's Hunting Directory arrives at the happiest conclusion. It reads—

"Strongly made hounds with a great deal of note and able to persevere without help are necessary for the country. This has been accomplished by the judicious crossing of English and American foxhounds."

It is of interest to note that as purveyors of a consistently high standard of sport the Green Spring Valley and its adjacent neighbour, the Elkridge Harford Hunt, stand second to none in America; and both packs are primarily composed of crossbred hounds.

However, there are certain factors affecting the type of hound required for some American countries which have no place in an English estimate. For instance—

a. It is common in the south, early and late in the season, to meet at 9.00 A.M. and go home at noon. With afternoon temperatures frequently rising into the eighties at these times of year this makes sense.

b. Some Hunts whose countries adjoin the big cities, e.g. the Potomac, the majority of whose members work in Washington D. C., very reasonably meet at 2.00 P.M. mid-week during the colder weather to allow their members to get out of their offices at lunch-time and on to their hunters. This sensible practice is worth consideration by similarly situated packs in England.

c. It is unusual to hunt in rain. As the weather, at least in the south, is usually fine and dry for long periods—rain and snow, when it does come, falling heavily and clearing quickly,—there seems, to the majority of fox-hunters in America, little point in exposing oneself to the discomforts of hunting in rain. If one observed this practice in the United Kingdom, one would get very little hunting at all. However, I sometimes question the sense of the British insistence on hunting in any weather, other than thick fog, with the mud in the field gateways up to our horses' bellies; it may do our souls good but it can play hell with our horses' legs.

I suggest that if you intend to hunt mostly short days and rarely in rain and mud, you do not need to go to the trouble and additional expense of breeding and keeping hounds of the conformation and stamina of English hounds. In England hounds must be bred to hunt over down and dale in pelting rain and holding mud for at least the five hours of the standard English hunting day and usually more, determined to kill their fox for every minute of it.

This determination probably stems from the fact—and it is a fact—that, in general, hounds in England expect to kill their fox; in general, hounds in America do not. A straightforward comparison of average tallies of foxes killed in any season proves this. However if endorsement of the fact is required we need look no further than the declared opinion of Thomas Allison, once huntsman of the Meadow Brook and one of the greatest American huntsmen of foxhounds. He had been born and bred to hunt the trencher-fed packs in Virginia and loved them. On moving north to become huntsman of the Meadowbrook Hunt in the state of New York, he had the opportunity to hunt the English hounds brought over by Mr David Dows and Mr Harry

Peters, Masters of the Meadow Brook. Of these hounds Allison said—

"Those English hounds . . . been bred to kill foxes, while our American hounds just hunts 'em. Twenty couple American hounds wouldn't break up a fox, not if you as't 'em. They'd bite him and call it a day. English hounds has judgment, speed, good noses and more stamina and they hunts to kill."

What Allison did not mention in this quotation, though I have no doubt he would have been the first to claim its' truth, is that the American hound will hunt generously for months without blood. They have of necessity been bred for generations to do this; the difficulty of killing their foxes allows no alternative.

Doubtless he would also claim that in the cold, dry, poor scenting conditions of the great Virginian woodland coverts the nose of the American hound will put that of the English sadly out of joint. This was most effectively demonstrated during the course of a match held in February 1968, between the American hounds of the Old Dominion Hunt of Virginia and the English hounds of the Hamilton Hunt of Canada, in the Old Dominion hunting country.

Despite the obvious advantage afforded the American hounds by the location of the contest, their ability to find and hunt a fox in the extremely difficult conditions existing during it—high winds, semi-drought and temperatures regularly as low as 15° Fahrenheit and never above freezing point—was so outstanding that the decision to award them the match was unanimously and wholeheartedly supported, even by their opponents.

The opinion of the two judges—of which I had the honour to be one—recorded that the superiority of the Old Dominion hounds in these particular conditions was so pre-eminent that the result would certainly have been the same had the match been held in any other hunting country in Virginia. Whether the American hounds would have done so well in the Hamilton Hunt country is another matter. It would be at least an interesting trial. On the only occasion recorded to date on which American hounds have been hunted outside America—in Ireland by the late very distinguished Master of Foxhounds, Mr Harry Worcester Smith—they found the weather and the terrain not to their liking. Irish hounds—knowing no other—seem able to cope.

So our fourth difference appears to lie in part in the approach to hunting of the huntsman, this in turn being dictated in part by the facts of life. In England it is necessary to kill foxes, in America it is not. A professional huntsman of American hounds of to-day asked how many foxes his hounds had killed in the past season replied—

"Reckon about a dozen or fifteen."

This would hardly be the answer of an English professional huntsman, expected to kill an average of fifty brace a season and proud of being able to do so. It was clear from the attitude of the American that he considered the killing of foxes unimportant in comparison to the sport his hounds showed hunting them.

Which is the cue for the next quotation.

"Kill our foxes! We don't kill our foxes! We love 'em!" (*Maryland cocktail party chatter*)

The English foxhunter will think this statement a little odd. But consider the facts. Few American hunting countries are contiguous to one another, and even those that are usually have some areas impossible to hunt. This combination encourages any game to gravitate to where it is the least disturbed; out of the country or inaccessible.

Secondly, the red fox is not native to the American continent, and, after his importation by hunting enthusiasts, has become indigenous only to the north eastern states and eastern Canada; though he can be found elsewhere in smaller numbers. Nowhere in America is he found in such strength as to require his numbers to be actively controlled by foxhunting as in England. The native is a grey fox, a dweller in swamps, round which he skulks when pursued by hounds, with no intention of quitting these safe havens. His finding is not greeted with any joyful anticipation of a fast thirty minutes and a six-mile point, and his killing is unworthy of note. Consequently, throughout most of the hunting countries the red fox is as carefully preserved as circumstances and the game laws permit. If and when he can be found, his loss to ground after, it is hoped, a good run, causes little grief, whereas his killing can be a cause of something near regret.

This practice would not commend itself to the fox-infested English farming community, and any English huntsman who observed it with any consistency would speedily be invited to seek other employment.

"The fox's best friend is the groundhog." (*disgruntled American foxhunter*)

Earth stopping as practised in England would probably be impossible in America. There are too many burrowing rodents and the biggest culprit is the groundhog or woodchuck—about the size of a small fox—which lives in colonies and a network of deep tunnels underneath open fields away from any woods. Riding over a Virginian hillside in which colonies of groundhog are resident has all the charm formerly associated with riding over a Sussex down riddled with rabbit holes in the days before myxamatosis. And more. The groundhog holes are bigger and deeper. Any fox going to ground in one of these caverns is impregnable to anything short of a nuclear weapon. Bolting him with a terrier or digging is out of the question. Thus, even if hounds do find a red fox, push him into the open and hold to him until they have him in view, it is still more than likely they will lose him to ground chez-groundhog.

"Everyone round here has his own dam pack of hounds." (*another Virginian MFH*)

Fox hunting, as we understand it in England, is practised by comparatively few Americans. The quotation may not appear to support this statement, but any American who has hunted in England—and this particular Virginian MFH had—will appreciate that it contains the very essence of this particular difference. And it is the most marked and saddest difference presently existing in the philosophy, circumstances and practice of fox hunting in America and England; the lack, in America, of wide local interest in and support for the local Hunt.

United States law permits, as I have mentioned, a greater freedom for any form of hunting. In consequence—and especially in the Virginia countryside, where fox hunting was first practised in America—any one can keep a few hunting hounds and many do. These the owner will hunt himself, by night and usually on foot, during the late summer or early autumn, where he chooses. The quality of these private packs varies from the excellent to the nondescript. The quarry for the better disciplined is the red or grey fox, or, for those hounds especially bred to hunt them, the racoon. However, by some ill-assorted miscellanies in which discipline is not all that could be desired, stray dog, cat, deer or anything else that turns up, which may include a courting couple or the owner of the property, can be hunted indiscriminately but rarely with malice aforethought.

The owner of these night-hounds—as they are customarily called—though he may breed horses, will rarely consider coming out with the Hunt. Nor is he, nor any country dweller who is not a subscriber in some form to the Hunt, usually interested enough to volunteer information to the huntsman on the whereabouts of the fox or hounds, even though they may have just crossed his path.

The Hunt is regarded by the majority of American countryfolk more as a competitor than as a co-operator in the destruction of vermin; and is certainly not the traditional cynosure of sporting and social interest in the local countryside as it is in most of the British Isles.

On hunting days, car, bicycle and foot followers are few. The local postmen, policemen and tradesmen do not arrange their rounds to coincide with the drawing of a particular covert. Though the English huntsman will not always trust the information he is offered by this customary multitude of supporters, he knows it is always available, along with every other possible form of assistance. His American counterpart is often sadly deprived, by lack of popular interest, of any such aid.

So to summarise. The American huntsman, having, let us say, bred to perfection the sort of hound he wants for his country, can be hindered in his hunting of it by the size and density of the coverts, the plethora of riot, the generally poor scenting conditions, the fewness of foxes, the multiplicity of bolt-holes, the depredations of the night-hunters and the lack of the traditionally strong, widespread, active support of the local countryfolk which we, in England, are all too apt to take for granted because we have never known it not to be so. A formidable array of discouragements.

But to counter these the American fox hunter has a considerable number of advantages enjoyed by few English Hunts. The American hunting countries, being largely permanent pasture, are excellent to ride and easy to get across over straightforward and inviting fences—mostly timber. There is little wire, and, where there is, efficient Hunt Committees install "chicken coops." The weather is rarely uncomfortable, the going is usually firm, even in the big woods, and there are fewer ' 'ard 'igh roads to 'ammer down." One rarely encounters the holding mud or hock-deep plough so common in Britain. This allows fox, hound and horse to move faster with less effort than would be the case over the average English countryside, and, as a result, the pace of a hunt is on average faster than in England; though, due to some of the hindrances listed above, it will usually on average be shorter. Finally, the American hunter is more often than not of thoroughbred American stock—ideally suited to the country. In over two seasons I have enjoyed seeing, and being permitted to ride, more hunters of real quality than I would have seen or ridden in hunting over a similar area in a season in England.

From these advantages of good going, good fences, good horses and good weather, together with a philosophic acceptance by fox hunter and hound of the difficulties involved, there seems to me to be in America a less ruthless, more unbusinesslike, relaxed attitude, an easier, gentler, pleasantly old-fashioned sense of the real enjoyment of fox hunting than exists sometimes in England to-day.

We English are often criticised for taking our pleasures sadly. Perhaps in our determination to keep up our tally of days hunted and foxes killed, come hell, hail, high water and the shades of night, some of us occasionally lose sight of the original purpose for which our forbears devised the sport of fox hunting. Fun.

People's Network